Ian St John's
BOOK OF SOCCER LISTS

Ian St John's
BOOK OF SOCCER LISTS

Ian St John
with Geoff Tibballs

CollinsWillow
An Imprint of HarperCollins*Publishers*

First published in 1992 by
CollinsWillow
an imprint of HarperCollins*Publishers*
London

A CIP catalogue record for this book
is available from the British Library

ISBN 0 00 218435 4

Printed and bound in Great Britain

CONTENTS

ACKNOWLEDGEMENTS

The assistance of the following is gratefully acknowledged in the preparation of this book: The Scottish Football Association, The Scottish Football League, The Scottish Football League Review, The Football Association, The GM Vauxhall Conference League, Trevor Spencer of Subbuteo, Ray Spiller, Niall MacSweeney, Barclays Bank, *Match* Magazine, ITV Sport and Kevin Flynn at the BBC. Among invaluable reference books was *The Football Grounds of Great Britain* by Simon Inglis (Collins Willow).

INTRODUCTION

Welcome to my Book of Soccer Lists. My mate Greavsie reckons that football's a 'funny old game' but of course it's also a fascinating game, littered with incredible facts and feats. Here I've compiled over 200 lists guaranteed to settle, or start, endless pub arguments. For example, who'd have thought that the first club in Scotland to instal floodlights would be tiny Stenhousemuir? And do you know which League club used to play at The Cow Pat? Or which club's fanzine is called *Mr. Bismarck's Electric Pickelhaube*? The lists cover every aspect of the game – domestic competitions (including non-league), players, managers, Europe and the World Cup. So you can find out the ten current League clubs with the worst records in the FA Cup; the ten clubs who have had most managers since the war; the ten clubs who have produced most internationals; the ten League grounds with the largest pitches; the last ten clubs to leave the Scottish League; and even the British grounds which are nearest to the sea. There's also a selection of oddballs including the ten best-selling (though not necessarily the most tuneful) football records from *Back Home* to *Blue Is The Colour*! And I can't be accused of favouritism. I've even included the day in 1959 when my old club Liverpool, then in the Second Division, were dumped out of the FA Cup by little Worcester City. But I hasten to add I wasn't playing for them then. So whether you support Arsenal or Altrincham, Manchester United or Montrose, I hope you'll find something here to set you thinking.

Ian St John

CHAPTER ONE
CLUB CALL

THE 10 MOST SUCCESSFUL ENGLISH CLUBS IN HISTORY

(League, FA Cup, League Cup, European Cup, European Cup Winners' Cup, Fairs/UEFA Cup)

		Trophies won
1.	Liverpool	33
2.	Aston Villa	18
3.	Arsenal	17
	Manchester United	17
5.	Tottenham Hotspur	15
6.	Everton	14
7.	Newcastle United	11
8.	Manchester City	9
	Nottingham Forest	9
	Wolverhampton Wanderers	9

I was lucky enough to be signed from Motherwell for £37,500 at the start of Liverpool's modern success story. But people forget that we only came out of the Second Division in 1961-62. Prior to that, the club had spent eight years in the Second, a period which included that infamous Cup defeat at the hands of little Worcester City and which also saw them suffer their record defeat, 9-1 against Birmingham City in December 1954. Of course, the man who turned everything round at Anfield was the great Bill Shankly. He lived and breathed football. I remember once there was a story going around that he'd taken his wife Nessie to watch Rochdale as an anniversary present. Shanks vehemently denied the rumours, saying: 'It was her birthday. Would I have got married during the football season? And anyway, it wasn't Rochdale – it was Rochdale Reserves!'

THE 30 MOST FREE-SCORING CLUBS IN FOOTBALL LEAGUE HISTORY

		goals per League game
1.	Bootle	2.227
2.	Barnet	1.928
3.	New Brighton Tower	1.902
4.	Burton Wanderers	1.855
5.	Darwen	1.728
6.	Liverpool	1.723
7.	Aston Villa	1.707
8.	Manchester United	1.675
	Tottenham Hotspur	1.675
10.	Wolverhampton Wanderers	1.668
11.	Manchester City	1.666
12.	Arsenal	1.659
13.	Everton	1.650
14.	Sunderland	1.632
15.	Nelson	1.621
16.	Bradford Park Avenue	1.605
17.	Derby County	1.601
18.	Newcastle United	1.597
19.	West Bromwich Albion	1.588
20.	Accrington Stanley	1.583
21.	Sheffield United	1.582
22.	Blackburn Rovers	1.571
23.	Luton Town	1.566
24.	Gateshead	1.563
25.	West Ham United	1.551
26.	Sheffield Wednesday	1.550
27.	Southampton	1.548
28.	Leicester City	1.543
29.	Wigan Borough	1.541
30.	Northampton Town	1.540

How about that? Two Merseyside teams in the top three and neither of them Everton or Liverpool. Nor even Tranmere. Bootle's other claim to fame is that they were the first club to resign from the Football League, which they did after being members for just one season, 1892-93. And in spite of their goalscoring exploits that year, they finished below half-way in Division Two since they contrived to let in 63 goals in their 22 games. New Brighton Tower lasted three seasons from 1898-1901 but the town was later represented by plain New Brighton. They joined the League in 1923 but were replaced by Workington in 1951.

THE 12 ORIGINAL FOOTBALL LEAGUE MEMBERS

Accrington
Aston Villa
Blackburn Rovers
Bolton Wanderers
Burnley
Derby County
Everton
Notts County
Preston North End
Stoke City
West Bromwich Albion
Wolverhampton Wanderers

The results for the opening day (8 September, 1888) were: Bolton 3, Derby 6; Everton 2, Accrington 1; Preston 5, Burnley 2; Stoke 0, West Brom 2; Wolves 1, Aston Villa 1. A crowd of 6,000 turned up to watch Preston and they went on to win the title without losing a game.

THE 30 MOST SHOT-SHY CLUBS IN FOOTBALL LEAGUE HISTORY

		goals per League game
1.	Loughborough Town	1.076
2.	Hereford United	1.204
3.	Merthyr Town	1.248
4.	Gainsborough Trinity	1.273
5.	Thames	1.274
6.	Workington	1.277
7.	Oxford United	1.284
	Halifax Town	1.284
9.	Leyton Orient	1.287
10.	Cambridge United	1.300
11.	Middlesbrough Ironopolis	1.321
12.	Aberdare Athletic	1.325
13.	Gillingham	1.339
14.	Glossop North End	1.341
15.	Southport	1.346
16.	New Brighton	1.347
17.	Hartlepool United	1.348
18.	Barrow	1.354
	Scarborough	1.354
20.	Burton United	1.357
21.	Rochdale	1.362
22.	Stalybridge Celtic	1.368
23.	Aldershot	1.371
24.	Crewe Alexandra	1.374
	Port Vale	1.374
26.	Shresbury Town	1.375
27.	Durham City	1.378
	Exeter City	1.378
29.	Scunthorpe United	1.379
30.	Newport County	1.385

Loughborough Town definitely go down as the worst team in the entire history of the Football League. They were members from 1895-1900 and, as we'll see from a later list, their inability to score naturally didn't win them too many matches. In their final season, they won just one game out of 34 and conceded 100 goals in the process. Yet their brief career did have a highspot. On 12 December 1896, a season that saw them reach the dizzy heights of fifth from bottom of Division Two (there were only two divisions in those days), Loughborough trounced Arsenal 8-0 in what would have been a real coupon-buster had the pools been invented then. Their victims were known at the time as Woolwich Arsenal and to this day, that remains the Gunners' heaviest defeat. Poor old Workington – they didn't always get their priorities right. In 1966, they had 13 directors and only 12 full-time players. Worse still, the directors could probably have beaten them.

WHAT'S IN A NAME

Many of today's clubs started out under a different name. Here are a few.

L & Y Railway FC (Manchester United)
Dial Square FC (Arsenal)
St Mary's YMCA (Southampton)
St Jude's Institute (Queen's Park Rangers)
Christ Church (Bolton Wanderers)
Pine Villa (Oldham Athletic)
Black Arabs (Bristol Rovers)
Singers FC (Coventry City)
Heaton Norris Rovers (Stockport County)
Thames Ironworks (West Ham United)
Small Heath Alliance (Birmingham City)
St Luke's (Wolverhampton Wanderers)
Ardwick (Manchester City)
St Domingo's FC (Everton)
New Brompton (Gillingham)
Belmont FC (Tranmere Rovers)
Boscombe St John's (Bournemouth)
Riverside FC (Cardiff City)
St Andrew's (Fulham)

Southampton were founded by a vicar, the Rev A.B. Sole, which is why they're known as the Saints. Bolton started out as a Sunday School team under the name of Christ Church but when the club committee and the vicar fell out, they had to quit the church. Being homeless and wanderers, they were promptly christened Bolton Wanderers. Their neighbours Manchester United were formed by a group of enthusiastic workers at the Newton Heath depot of the Lancashire and Yorkshire Railway and quickly changed their name from L & Y Railway to Newton Heath. In those days, their players used to change in a pub and had to walk a few hundred yards to the ground. Good job Georgie Best wasn't playing for them then – he might never have made it to the match! I remember when Liverpool played the great United team of the 1960 s and beforehand Shanks, who loved to tell us that the opposition were rubbish, took them apart one by one. He came out with comments like 'Alex Stepney – couldn't catch a cold; somebody told me Matt Busby has a bad back, I'll tell you he's got two bad backs; I've seen a juggernaut turn quicker than Billy Foulkes; and Paddy Crerand. Now boys, Crerand's deceptive – he's slower than you think.' He said we only had three players to beat – Law, Best and Charlton. 'And if you can't do that, you don't deserve to be professional footballers.' It was a terrific build-up, we felt we could conquer the world. United beat us 4-0!

FOOTBALL LEAGUE CLUBS WITH MOST SEASONS IN DIVISION ONE

(up to and including Premier League 1992-93)

		seasons
1	Everton	90
2.	Aston Villa	83
3.	Liverpool	78
4.	Arsenal	76
5.	Sunderland	70
6.	Manchester City	69
7.	Manchester United	68
	West Bromwich Albion	68
9.	Newcastle United	63
10.	Sheffield Wednesday	62

Everton have only been relegated twice in their history. In 1930, they went down for one season despite amassing a respectable 35 points from 42 games and scoring 80 goals, more than fifth-placed Leeds. And in 1951, Chelsea's superior goal difference sent Everton and Sheffield Wednesday tumbling into the Second from which Everton were duly promoted again three years later. For their part, Arsenal have never been relegated since they stopped being with the 'Woolwich' in 1913. It's hardly surprising that those north-east giants, Sunderland and Newcastle, consider their rightful place to be in the top flight with 133 seasons between them but they're by no means the only ones to have slipped from grace. Bolton with 60, Burnley with 51 and Preston with 46 seasons have all enjoyed long spells in the First Division. The Bolton side of the Fifties was notoriously tough. Their left-back Doug Hennin used to tell his team-mates: 'If my inside-forward 'appens to come through, chip him back to me...'

FOOTBALL LEAGUE CLUBS WITH MOST CURRENT SEASONS IN DIVISION ONE

(including Premier League 1992-93)

1.	Arsenal	67
2.	Everton	39
3.	Liverpool	31
4.	Coventry City	26
5.	Manchester United	18
6.	Nottingham Forest	16
7.	Southampton	15
	Tottenham Hotspur	15
9.	Queen's Park Rangers	10
10.	Norwich City	7
	Wimbledon	7

Despite what seems like an annual battle against relegation (only three times have they finished higher than tenth), Coventry City hold the distinction of being the only club in the top flight never to have been relegated from the old First Division. They were promoted in 1967 yet just eight years earlier, had been languishing in the Fourth Division. Their surge up the League coincided with the appointment of a certain Jimmy Hill as manager. He brought in all sorts of innovations – Radio Sky Blue (with former England wicket-keeper Godfrey Evans as disc jockey!), the Sky Blue News, a new concept in match-day programmes, and an electric scoreboard, donated by the local paper. It reminds me of a classic gaffe Jimmy once made on Match of the Day. It was late on Saturday night and British Summer Time was due to end the following day. Jimmy's closing words were: 'Good night. And don't forget tonight to put your cocks back.'

THE 20 CLUBS WITH MOST FOOTBALL LEAGUE GOALS IN HISTORY

(up to the end of 1991-92)

1.	Aston Villa	6247
2.	Wolverhampton Wanderers	6155
3.	Liverpool	6071
4.	Everton	6018
5.	Manchester United	5956
6.	Manchester City	5929
7.	Sunderland	5925
8.	Derby County	5874
9.	Arsenal	5845
10.	West Bromwich Albion	5844
11.	Blackburn Rovers	5812
12.	Sheffield United	5677
13.	Newcastle United	5661
14.	Preston North End	5629
15.	Burnley	5628
16.	Bolton Wanderers	5605
17.	Sheffield Wednesday	5557
18.	Notts County	5505
19.	Grimsby Town	5449
20.	Leicester City	5445

The fastest goal in Aston Villa's League history was the one scored by their left-half Bob Iverson in a home game against Charlton on 3 December 1938. It came after just ten seconds and the only Charlton player to touch the ball was legendary goalkeeper Sam Bartram. Mind you, they didn't hang about in the final game of last season, at home to Coventry. Cyrille Regis headed them in front after just 20 seconds – and it might have been even quicker if Coventry hadn't kicked off.

THE 10 YOUNGEST CURRENT FOOTBALL LEAGUE CLUBS

		Founded
1.	Colchester United	1937
2.	Peterborough United	1934
3.	Wigan Athletic	1932
4.	Hereford United	1924
5.	York City	1922
6.	Cambridge United	1919
	Leeds United	1919
8.	Swansea City	1912
9.	Halifax Town	1911
10.	Hartlepool United	1908
	Huddersfield Town	1908

Colchester may be officially the babies of the League but it could be that something resembling football was played in the region long before. For 17 th century records tell of a game with the dubious title of 'camping' which was described as an 'athletic game of ball in vogue in the Eastern Counties, especially on the borders of Suffolk.' For their part, the rise of Huddersfield Town was nothing short of incredible since in the early days, conditions at Leeds Road were so primitive that the dressing rooms were in an old tramcar. The club first joined the North-Eastern League but couldn't afford the travelling costs and so in 1909 gained admission to the Midland League. They then applied to join Division Two of the Football League and, remarkably just two years after being formed, they were accepted. But immediately after the First World War, in 1919, Huddersfield Town nearly folded and it was only the intervention of the supporters' committee that prevented the club from being merged with the newly-formed Leeds United. All that was forgotten by 1922 when they won the FA Cup and, initially under the guidance of the great Herbert Chapman, won the Championship for a then record three years in succession between 1924 and 1926. They also finished runners-up the following two years. Who says there are no such things as fairy stories?

THE 10 OLDEST CURRENT FOOTBALL LEAGUE CLUBS

		Founded
1.	Notts County	1862
2.	Stoke City	1863
3.	Nottingham Forest	1865
4.	Chesterfield	1866
5.	Sheffield Wednesday	1867
6.	Reading	1871
7.	Wrexham	1873
8.	Aston Villa	1874
	Bolton Wanderers	1874
10.	Birmingham City	1875
	Blackburn Rovers	1875

The oldest Association Football Club of all is actually Sheffield FC, formed in 1855, but Notts County lay claim to being the oldest Football League club even though most of their early matches took place on cricket grounds. In fact, when they became founder members of the League in 1888, their home was Trent Bridge. But cricket still took priority there which meant that come April and September, County had to find somewhere else to play their home matches. Neighbours Nottingham Forest were originally formed not to play football, but a game called 'shinney' which was a type of hockey. Besides being the third-oldest League club, Forest have another claim to fame. It was at their old ground, the Forest Racecourse, that the shrill blast of a referee's whistle was first heard in 1878 in a game against Sheffield Norfolk. For their part, Sheffield Wednesday grew out of a cricket club, so called because its members only played on their afternoon off, a Wednesday.

CLUBS WHO HAVE SUPPLIED MOST FULL ENGLAND INTERNATIONALS

1. Aston Villa   53
2. Everton   50
3. Arsenal   45
   Tottenham Hotspur   45
5. West Bromwich Albion   41
6. Liverpool   39
7. Manchester United   38
8. Blackburn Rovers   37
   Sheffield Wednesday   37
10. Derby County   35
11. Nottingham Forest   33
12. Sheffield United   32
    Wolverhampton Wanderers   32
14. Manchester City   31
15. Chelsea   30

Aston Villa's most remarkable cap was right-half Jack Reynolds, the only player ever to score deliberately for and against England. As a player with Distillery, he had won five caps for Ireland and had scored against England in 1890 despite being injured early on in the match. Then in 1892, he was capped by England (the selectors clearly being less fussy about birth qualifications than Jack Charlton) and, while with first West Brom and then Villa, proceeded to score three goals in eight internationals for his new country. He didn't score against Ireland though. Everton left-back Ray Wilson was one of the unsung heroes of England's 1966 World Cup winning team. But thanks to me, he didn't have the best of starts to his international career. After only 15 minutes of his debut against Scotland in 1960 (he was playing for Huddersfield then), he and I went for a ball, my knee caught him in the face and he ended up with a broken nose. It was a pure accident though. Ray's an undertaker now – he always was good around the box.

CURRENT LEAGUE CLUBS WHO HAVE NEVER SUPPLIED A FULL INTERNATIONAL

Barnet
Colchester United
Darlington
Halifax Town
Rochdale
Scarborough
Scunthorpe United
Torquay United
Wigan Athletic

Even though none of their players has been capped while actually with them, these clubs have managed to produce players who have gone on to earn international status with other teams. Take Kevin Keegan and Ray Clemence who both started out at Scunthorpe, Geoff Thomas at Rochdale and Lee Sharpe at Torquay. On leaving school and before turning professional, Kevin Keegan was employed as a clerk at a Doncaster brass works. Ironically, for ages he couldn't get into the firm's first team at football, being kept out by an assortment of fitters and welders, and he had to bide his time in the reserves. Among the clubs who have produced just one international are Stockport County. They threw up England goalkeeper Harry Hardy who, on his solitary appearance against Belgium in 1924, kept a clean sheet as England won 4-0. Alas he was never asked back.

LEAST SUCCESSFUL FOOTBALL LEAGUE CUP TEAMS

The following clubs have never progressed beyond the third round:

Barnet
Crewe Alexandra
Hereford United
Port Vale
Scarborough
Scunthorpe United
Southend United
Torquay United

G reavsie won't be too thrilled to see Southend's name on this list but surely the distinction for being the least successful Football League Cup team of all must go to Port Vale. In 32 years of competition, they had never got past the second round until last season. And when they did finally reach the third round, they had the misfortune to meet Liverpool. Along with Nottingham Forest, Liverpool share the record for the most League Cup triumphs with four. Liverpool won the competition four years in a row between 1981 and 1984 during which time they went a record 24 games without defeat between losing 1-0 at Bradford City in August 1980 and 1-0 at Burnley in February 1983. Even then, these ties were two-legged affairs and Liverpool went through on aggregate.

NON FIRST DIVISION WINNERS OF THE FOOTBALL LEAGUE CUP

Norwich City	Division 2	1962
Queen's Park Rangers	Division 3	1967
Swindon Town	Division 3	1969
Aston Villa	Division 2	1975
Sheffield Wednesday	Division 2	1991

The smaller clubs have a pretty good record in the League Cup. Fourth Division Rochdale reached the second final in 1962 and in 1974-75, little Chester, also then in the Fourth, got to the semi-finals before narrowly going down 5-4 on aggregate to Aston Villa. And who could forget how Queen's Park Rangers, inspired by the wizardry of Rodney Marsh, fought back to defeat West Brom 3-2 in the 1967 final or how, two years later, Don Rogers and Swindon Town shattered mighty Arsenal 3-1? Incidentally, Rangers' triumph was in the first final to be played at Wembley – previous finals had been over two legs. The man who guided Sheffield Wednesday to success in 1991 was Ron Atkinson, a man journalists can always rely on for a snappy quote. When he became Manchester United manager ten years earlier, Big Ron told pressmen that they were welcome to his home phone number 'but please remember not to ring me during The Sweeney'. He often has more silverware on his wrists than most clubs have in their trophy cabinets but after being sacked by United, he lamented: 'I've had to swap my Merc for a BMW, I'm down to my last 37 suits and I'm drinking non-vintage champagne.' It's a tough life.

THE LAST 15 CLUBS TO LEAVE THE FOOTBALL LEAGUE

(not including automatic relegation)

1.	Maidstone United	August 1992
2.	Aldershot	March 1992
3.	Southport	1978
4.	Workington	1977
5.	Barrow	1972
6.	Bradford Park Avenue	1970
7.	Accrington Stanley	1962
8.	Gateshead	1960
9.	New Brighton	1951
10.	Gillingham	1938
11.	Thames	1932
	Wigan Borough	1932
13.	Newport County	1931*
	Nelson	1931
15.	Merthyr Tydfil	1930

It's always sad when, for whatever reason, a club has to quit the League. But perhaps the least mourned of the dearly departed were Thames who were replaced by the ill-fated Newport County in 1932. Thames only played in the Football League for two years and their home ground was the old West Ham Greyhound Stadium. They must have known they were going to the dogs when only 469 spectators turned up to see them play Luton in 1930, the lowest attendance for a Saturday afternoon League fixture in history.

* Newport re-joined the League in 1932

THE LAST 10 CLUBS TO JOIN THE FOOTBALL LEAGUE

(Not including those re-joining via promotion from the Conference)

1.	Barnet	1991
2.	Maidstone United	1989
3.	Scarborough	1987
4.	Wigan Athletic	1978
5.	Wimbledon	1977
6.	Hereford United	1972
7.	Cambridge United	1970
8.	Oxford United	1962
9.	Peterborough United	1960
10.	Workington	1951

There's no doubt which of those clubs has made the biggest impact: It has to be the Wombles of Wimbledon, the self-styled Crazy Gang. Just 11 seasons after stepping up from non-league football, they won the FA Cup itself, beating Liverpool 1-0. Before the final, their winger Wally Downes came out with the classic remark: 'Wimbledon will take to Wembley. Once you've tried to get a decent bath at Hartlepool, you can handle anything.' Although he'd left by the time they won the Cup, manager Dave Bassett was Wimbledon's guiding light. Like Ron Atkinson, Dave is good with the one-liners. He once described Wimbledon as 'the borstal of football' and when Dons fans attempted a mini pitch invasion to mark promotion to the First Division, Bassett told reporters: 'The only hooligans here are the players.' And it was Bassett who, in the club's Fourth Division days, told his players after one match that they were nothing but a bunch of clowns and amateurs, and that's why they'd never reach the top. Twenty minutes later, the team van ground to a halt on the M4. Dave had forgotten to fill it up with petrol.

THE 6 WORST BEHAVED FOOTBALL LEAGUE TEAMS (1991-92)

		Sent off	Booked	Total
1.	Southampton	5	80	85
2.	Exeter City	5	67	72
3.	Lincoln City	8	61	69
	Stoke City	2	67	69
5.	Scunthorpe United	5	62	67
6.	Millwall	2	63	65

Some Saints! But they had nothing on winger Willie Johnston who was sent off a record 15 times in his career between 1969 and 1983 – seven times with Rangers, four with West Brom, twice with Hearts and once each playing for Vancouver Whitecaps and Scotland. Even Willie usually managed to last longer on the pitch than Wrexham's Ambrose Brown who was dismissed after just 20 seconds of the Third Division (North) fixture with Hull City in 1936 – the Football League's quickest sending-off. I had a few brushes with referees too. Once I was sent off at Coventry after a fracas. It was a few days before a vital cup-tie and Shanks, trying to make sure I was available for the cup game, set about doctoring the evidence. He got Bob Paisley to apply a mixture of gentian violet and black boot polish around my private parts and then invited the press in for (not too close) a look. On the Monday, the papers were full of the brutal attack on Ian St John which had caused the brawl. Shanks was sure the FA disciplinary committee, which met that day, would clear me for the cup tie but instead I was suspended for 14 days. I had lost my case and my dignity!

THE 5 BEST BEHAVED FOOTBALL LEAGUE TEAMS (1991-92)

		Sent off	Booked	Total
1.	Ipswich Town	1	22	23
	Norwich City	1	22	23
3.	Everton	0	24	24
	Oldham Athletic	0	24	24
5.	Portsmouth	3	22	25

I pswich have always been a friendly club. That family spirit used to be epitomised by their late chairman, John Cobbold, known to all as 'Mister John'. His equally charming brother Patrick once defined a crisis at Ipswich Town as being when the boardroom has run out of white wine...

MOST FOOTBALL LEAGUE DIVISION ONE CHAMPIONSHIPS

1.	Liverpool	18
2.	Arsenal	10
3.	Everton	9
4.	Aston Villa	7
	Manchester United	7
6.	Sunderland	6
7.	Newcastle United	4
	Sheffield Wednesday	4
9.	Huddersfield Town	3
	Leeds United	3
	Wolverhampton Wanderers	3

THE 9 CHAMPIONSHIP RUNNERS-UP WHO HAVE YET TO WIN THE TITLE

Bristol City (1906-07)
Oldham Athletic (1914-15)
Cardiff City (1923-24)
Leicester City (1928-29)
Charlton Athletic (1936-37)
Blackpool (1955-56)
Queen's Park Rangers (1975-76)
Watford (1982-83)
Southampton (1983-84)

The closest to glory were Cardiff, beaten on goal average by Huddersfield. Their goal differences were identical (27) – Huddersfield's being 60-33 and Cardiff's 61-34. Indeed had goal difference been the deciding system in those days, Cardiff would surely have won the title by virtue of having scored one goal more. As if all that wasn't enough to douse the dragon's fire, Cardiff would have been champions anyway had they not missed a penalty in their final match. Oldham, Leicester and Queen's Park Rangers all missed the title by a solitary point, to Everton, The Wednesday and Liverpool respectively. Managed by Graham Taylor, the Watford team of the early 1980s didn't win too many friends with their brand of direct football. Critics claimed Watford did for soccer what Lester Piggott has done for after-dinner speaking while Terry Venables reckoned they were setting English football back ten years. Some might argue that means Stanley Matthews is due for a recall any day...

MOST RELEGATED FOOTBALL LEAGUE CLUBS

1.	Notts County	12
2.	Birmingham City	10
	Bolton Wanderers	10
	Grimsby Town	10
	Preston North End	10
6.	Cardiff City	9
	Sheffield Wednesday	9
8.	Bristol City	8
	Burnley	8
	Bury	8
	Derby County	8
	Doncaster Rovers	8
	Leicester City	8
	Manchester City	8
	Sheffield United	8
	Wolverhampton Wanderers	8
17.	Bradford City	7
	Hull City	7
	Lincoln City	7
	Middlesbrough	7
	Port Vale	7
	Stoke City	7
	Swansea City	7
	West Bromwich Albion	7

The most spectacular declines were those of Bristol City and Wolves who both plunged from the First Division to the Fourth in successive seasons, City 1979-82 and Wolves 1983-86. The irrepressible Tommy Docherty was one of Wolves' managers during that period. In the middle of one particularly bad goal drought, he reckoned that Wolves were no longer using a stopwatch to judge their golden goal competition – instead they were using a calendar.

MOST APPLICATIONS FOR
RE-ELECTION

1.	Hartlepool United	14
2.	Halifax Town	12
3.	Barrow	11
	Southport	11
5.	Crewe Alexandra	10
	Newport County	10
	Rochdale	10
8.	Darlington	8
	Exeter City	8
10.	Chester City	7
	Walsall	7
	Workington	7
	York City	7
15.	Stockport County	6
16.	Accrington Stanley	5
	Gillingham	5
	Lincoln City	5
	New Brighton	5
20.	Bradford P. A.	4
	Northampton Town	4
	Norwich City	4

When Hartlepool entertained Wimbledon once, visiting keeper Dave Beasant found a different sort of object being thrown at him – a Mars bar. He picked it up, thanked the fans behind the goal and put it in his glove bag. Shortly afterwards, wandering to the edge of his area, he heard an almighty cheer from behind. He turned round to see a small boy in the back of the net reclaiming his Mars bar!

BOGEY TEAMS – LONGEST LEAGUE RUNS WITHOUT VICTORY

		Matches	
1.	COVENTRY CITY v Aston Villa	26	(1937-88)
2.	BLACKPOOL v Arsenal	24	(1896-1937)
3.	CARLISLE UNITED v Hull City	23	(1930-63)
4.	ASTON VILLA v Tottenham Hotspur	22	(1938-62)
	SUNDERLAND v Liverpool	22	(1958-81)
6.	HALIFAX TOWN v York City	21	(1939-56)
7.	HUDDERSFIELD TOWN v Arsenal	20	(1927-37)
	PORT VALE v Walsall	20	(1965-86)
	ROCHDALE v Brentford	20	(1958-date)
	SHEFFIELD UNITED v Huddersfield	20	(1929-54)

Every club has its bogey teams and grounds – Spurs went 38 League matches, a period spanning 73 years, before winning at Anfield in 1985. Shanks used to call Spurs 'The Drury Lane Fan Dancers' because he thought they were a soft touch. And whilst Coventry have always struggled against Aston Villa, City's Highfield Road ground was a veritable graveyard for Norwich. The Canaries lost 19 League games on the trot there between 1937 and 1980. Equally, Leicester must have dreaded the trip to Stamford Bridge – they lost 15 in a row there over a spell of 54 years. The jinx was finally broken in 1960. Chesterfield went 62 years (27 matches) without winning at Stockport (eventually triumphing there in 1962); Swindon suffered 56 years of pain at Gillingham (not winning in 27 matches, 1930-86); and Manchester City also went 27 games, a period of 54 years, without winning at Sheffield Wednesday. But most remarkable of all is the fact that Luton have never picked up so much as a point at Old Trafford. In all, they have made 18 fruitless visits dating back to season 1897-98.

FAVOURITE OPPOSITION – LONGEST RUNS OF CONSECUTIVE LEAGUE WINS

		Matches	
1.	PORTSMOUTH v Everton	13	(1946-56)
	QUEEN'S PARK RANGERS v Walsall	13	(1929-52)
3.	CHARLTON ATHLETIC v Bristol City	12	(1931-65)
	COLCHESTER UNITED v Crewe	12	(1965-77)
5.	ARSENAL v Middlesbrough	11	(1930-36)
	BIRMINGHAM CITY v Luton Town	11	(1897-1951)
	CHESTER CITY v Hartlepool United	11	(1934-47)
	STOCKPORT COUNTY v Barrow	11	(1921-31)

Four clubs have notched up seven consecutive away League victories on their favourite grounds – Derby at Wolves between 1908 and 1926; Everton at Liverpool (1908-19); Newcastle at Derby (1950-69); and Spurs at Aston Villa (1938-57). Everton certainly enjoyed the better of the Merseyside derbies in the early part of the century – in all, they had a 15-match unbeaten run at Anfield in the League. At Liverpool, the trip we always looked forward to was Sunderland. Indeed Liverpool's last League defeat at Roker Park was back in August 1958, 16 matches ago. Also worth a mention are Birmingham, who went 15 League games unbeaten at Nottingham Forest between 1914 and 1961, and Brighton who went 15 undefeated at Aldershot between 1935 and 1964. Even the lowly have their moments. Accrington Stanley won 16 home games on the trot against Darlington between 1927 and 1951 while Mansfield performed a similar feat against Halifax between 1932 and 1959. Aston Villa also won 16 in a row at home, their perennial victims being Sheffield United between 1901 and 1922. Leicester gained 15 successive home League victories over Blackpool (1896-1913) and, like many clubs before and after, Gillingham submitted meekly in the Lion's Den, losing 15 in a row at Millwall between 1926 and 1959. The Gills finally stopped the rot with a hard-earned draw – I bet it made Brian Moore's day.

HIGHEST PERCENTAGE OF WINS IN FOOTBALL LEAGUE HISTORY

(not including play-offs)

1.	Barnet	50.0
2.	New Brighton Tower	47.0
3.	Liverpool	46.8
4.	Burton Wanderers	46.7
5.	Manchester United	44.1
6.	Arsenal	43.6
7.	Stalybridge Celtic	43.5
8.	Aston Villa	42.5
9.	Tottenham Hotspur	42.2
10.	Everton	42.1
11.	Wolverhampton Wanderers	41.5
12.	Ipswich Town	41.2
13.	Leeds United	41.1
	Manchester City	41.1
	Wimbledon	41.1
16.	Sunderland	41.0
17.	Newcastle United	40.7
	Wigan Athletic	40.7
19.	Sheffield United	40.2
20.	Brighton & Hove Albion	40.1
21.	Reading	40.0
22.	Queen's Park Rangers	39.8
23.	Peterborough United	39.7
	Sheffield Wednesday	39.7
25.	Derby County	39.6

Barnet have got a lot to live up to in their second season. Even so, I don't think they'll be calling Greavsie out of retirement just yet. He enjoyed his days at Underhill, particularly since chairman Stan Flashman could lay his hands on tickets for just about anything, even a Buckingham Palace garden party. Flashman's mentor in ticket touting was Johnny Goldstein who used to be a great Spurs fan. When he died, all the Spurs first-teamers went to the funeral. Fittingly, it was all-ticket.

LOWEST PERCENTAGE OF WINS IN FOOTBALL LEAGUE HISTORY

(not including play-offs)

1.	Loughborough Town	21.5
2.	Thames	23.8
3.	Northwich Victoria	24.0
4.	Merthyr Town	27.4
5.	Middlesbrough Ironopolis	28.6
6.	Burton United	30.4
7.	Aberdare Athletic	30.9
8.	Gainsborough Trinity	31.0
9.	Glossop North End	31.9
	Halifax Town	31.9
11.	Maidstone United	32.1
12.	Workington	32.2
13.	Darwen	32.3
14.	Barrow	32.4
15.	New Brighton	32.5
16.	Hereford United	32.7
17.	Rochdale	32.9
	Southport	32.9
19.	Ashington	33.2
	Durham City	33.2
	Newport County	33.2
22.	Crewe Alexandra	33.5
23.	Aldershot	33.6
	Hartlepool United	33.6
	Leyton Orient	33.6

Poor old Loughborough again! There are some grand old names in this list Imagine being a Middlesborough Ironopolis supporter and chanting, 'Give us an M!' Merthyr Town were the forerunners of Merthyr Tydfil and in 1921 drew over 21,000 to Penydarren Park for a game with Millwall. And with a population of only 25,000, Glossop holds the distinction of being the smallest town ever to have supported an English First Division team. North End were in the top flight for just one season (1899-1900), finishing bottom.

34

FOOTBALL LEAGUE CLUBS WHO HAVE HAD POINTS DEDUCTED

	Pts deducted
Sunderland (1890-91)	2
Stockport County (1926-27)	2
Peterborough United (1967-68)	19
Preston North End (1973-74)	1
Newport County (1973-74)	1
Aldershot (1974-75)	1
Bristol Rovers (1981-82)	2
Mansfield Town (1981-82)	2
Tranmere Rovers (1987-88)	2
Halifax Town (1987-88)	1
Arsenal (1990-91)	2
Manchester United (1990-91)	1

The punishment meted out to Manchester United and Arsenal was the first concerning on-the-field activities. Both clubs were also fined £50,000 following the infamous brawl at Old Trafford. Apart from United, Arsenal, Tranmere, who had points deducted for failing to fulfil a fixture, and Peterborough, all the remaining clubs in the list were punished for fielding ineligible players. Peterborough were hit following financial irregularities and the 19 points they had deducted was deliberately designed to put them at the foot of Division Three and thus ensure relegation to the Fourth. So in effect they were relegated a division. Similarly in 1990, Swindon Town, after gaining promotion to Division One for the first time in their history, were forced to remain in the Second after being found guilty of making illegal payments. Two clubs have been expelled from the Football League – Leeds City in 1919 following allegations of irregular payments during wartime matches, and Port Vale in 1968, also for irregular payments. Vale successfully applied to rejoin but Leeds City were disbanded and a new club Leeds United was formed. Ironically when City were expelled, their fixtures were taken over by Burslem Port Vale...

MOST FOOTBALL LEAGUE GOALS SCORED IN A SEASON

1.	Peterborough United (1960-61, D4)	134
2.	Aston Villa (1930-31, D1)	128
	Bradford City (1928-29, D3 N)	128
4.	Arsenal (1930-31, D1)	127
	Millwall (1927-28, D3 S)	127
6.	Doncaster Rovers (1946-47, D3 N)	123
7.	Middlesbrough (1926-27, D2)	122
8.	Everton (1930-31, D2)	121
	Lincoln City (1951-52, D3 N)	121
10.	Arsenal (1932-33, D1)	118
	Barnsley (1933-34, D3 N)	118
12.	Everton (1931-32, D1)	116
	Barrow (1933-34, D3N)	116
14.	Wolverhampton Wanderers (1931-32, D2)	115
	Stockport County (1933-34, D3N)	115
	Arsenal (1934-35, D1)	115
	Tottenham Hotspur (1960-61, D1)	115

Peterborough's rise to power was little short of irresistible. They were members of the Midland League, the route to Football League status previously trodden by the likes of Barnsley, Chesterfield, Doncaster, Lincoln, Rotherham, Scunthorpe and Shrewsbury. Their FA Cup exploits in the Fifties were legendary. They disposed of League opponents on no fewer than eight occasions while in the Midland League itself, they lost just one home game between 1955 and 1960, averaging over four goals a game. They carried on when they were elected to the Football League in 1960 to replace Gateshead, their remarkable attacking exploits spearheaded by 52-goal Terry Bly. Another great goalscorer was Villa's lanky Tom Waring, nicknamed 'Pongo' after a popular cartoon dog of the time. He lived up to his canine image, being a great sniffer-out of goals (49 in Villa's record-breaking year), although there is no truth in the rumour that he buried his England caps in the back garden.

FEWEST FOOTBALL LEAGUE GOALS SCORED IN A SEASON

1. Loughborough Town (1899-1900, D2)   18
2. Darwen (1898-99, D2)   22
3. Doncaster Rovers (1904-05, D2)   23
4. Loughborough Town (1897-98, D2)   24
   Watford (1971-72, D2)   24
   Stoke City (1984-85, D1)   24
7. Stoke City (1888-89)   26
   Crewe Alexandra (1894-95, D2)   26
   Woolwich Arsenal (1912-13, D1)   26
   Swansea City (1974-75, D4)   26
   Leicester City (1977-78, D1)   26
12. Stoke City (1889-90)   27
   Lincoln City (1896-97, D2)   27
   Stockport County (1969-70, D3)   27
   Huddersfield Town (1971-72, D1)   27
   Wolverhampton Wanderers (1983-84, D1)   27
   Watford (1987-88, D1)   27

Inevitably the record for the fewest victories in a season belongs to our old friends Loughborough. They managed just one in 1899-1900 and were promptly kicked out of the League. Darwen only managed two wins in 1898-99, as did Rochdale when they finished bottom of Division Three in 1973-74. The miserly sum of three victories in a season was achieved by Stoke City (1889-90), Northwich Victoria in Division Two (1893-94), Crewe Alexandra (1894-95), Doncaster Rovers (1904-05), Woolwich Arsenal (1912-13), Fourth Division Southport (1976-77) and Stoke again in 1984-85. When they have a bad season in the Potteries, there are certainly no half measures!

WHAT'S IN A NAME – MORE FORMER CLUB NAMES

Glyn Cricket and Football Club (Leyton Orient)
Stanley (Newcastle United)
Headington United (Oxford United)
Thornhill United (Rotherham United)
Brumby Hall (Scunthorpe United)
West Herts (Watford)
Bristol South End (Bristol City)
Abbey United (Cambridge United)
Shaddowgate United (Carlisle United)
Sunderland and District Teachers AFC (Sunderland)

Sunderland's existence was down to one James Allan, a Scottish schoolteacher working at the town's Hendon Boarding School. He formed Sunderland and District Teachers AFC for the recreation and amusement of its members but financial problems (notably the £10 a year rent on their ground which was adjacent to a pub) forced them to admit members from outside the teaching profession, and so the name was changed to Sunderland AFC. Neighbours Newcastle were born out of two clubs involved in a bitter rivalry – West End and East End. West End had a ground, St James' Park, but East End had the team. The solution was for East End to play on West End's ground and thus, with the hatchet finally buried, Newcastle United were elected to the Football League in 1893. One of the principal characters in Watford's early days was a guy named Joey Goodchild who used to delight in climbing on to the stand roof of their old Cassio Road ground to do a tap dance for the crowd. But once the happy hoofer fell off the roof and landed on a lady. The club had to fork out £25 in compensation to the unfortunate woman and that was the end of Joey's dancing career.

MOST FOOTBALL LEAGUE GOALS
CONCEDED IN A SEASON

1.	Darwen (1898-99, D2)	141
2.	Nelson (1927-28, D3 N)	136
3.	Merthyr Town (1929-30, D3 S)	135
	Rochdale (1931-32, D3 N)	135
5.	Newport County (1946-47, D2)	133
6.	Blackpool (1930-31, D1)	125
7.	Accrington Stanley (1959-60, D3)	123
8.	Bradford Park Avenue (1955-56, D3 N)	122
9.	Ipswich Town (1963-64, D1)	121
10.	Charlton Athletic (1956-57, D1)	120
11.	Walsall (1952-53, D3S)	118
12.	Barrow (1926-27, D3N)	117
	Doncaster Rovers (1966-67, D3)	117
14.	Hartlepool (1932-33, D3N)	116
15.	Ashington (1928-29, D3N)	115
	Manchester United (1930-31, D1)	115
	Tranmere Rovers (1960-61, D3)	115

During that fateful season, Darwen suffered the indignity of three 10-0 defeats in the space of six weeks – against Manchester City, Walsall and, of all people, Loughborough Town. Ipswich's demise in 1963-64 came just two years after their shock championship success and followed Alf Ramsey's departure to manage England. Of course, Ramsey was a classy full-back in his playing days although Barnsley fanatic Michael Parkinson remembers him getting a real roasting from winger Johnny Kelly when Southampton visited Oakwell in the 1950 s. As Kelly skinned Ramsey for the umpteenth time, one of the locals called out: 'Ramsey – tha's as much use as a chocolate teapot.'

FEWEST FOOTBALL LEAGUE GOALS CONCEDED IN A SEASON

1.	Preston North End (1888-89)	15
2.	Liverpool (1978-79, D1)	16
3.	Arsenal (1990-91, D1)	18
	Liverpool (1893-94, D2)	18
5.	Sheffield United (1892-93, D2)	19
6.	Port Vale (1953-54, D3 N)	21
	Southampton (1921-22, D3 S)	21
	Stockport County (1921-22, D3 N)	21
9.	Wednesday (1899-1900, D2)	22
	Woolwich Arsenal (1903-04, D2)	22
11.	Preston North End (1890-91)	23
	Manchester United (1924-25, D2)	23
13.	Burnley (1897-98, D2)	24
	Small Heath (1900-01, D2)	24
	Middlesbrough (1901-02, D2)	24
	Preston North End (1903-04, D2)	24
	Plymouth Argyle (1921-22, D3S)	24
	Birmingham City (1947-48, D2)	24
	Liverpool (1970-71, D1)	24
	Nottingham Forrest (1977-78, D1)	24
	Crystal Palace (1978-79, D2)	24
	Liverpool (1987-88, D1)	24

Preston's 'Invincibles' carried all before them in the Football League's inaugural year, not only winning the title without losing a game but also the FA Cup without conceding a goal. However, they did only play 22 matches in the League so in truth the more recent feats of the likes of Liverpool (42 games) and Arsenal (38) are worthier still. Liverpool conceded just four goals at Anfield in 1978-79 which prompted Bob Paisley to remark: 'Mind, I've been here during the bad times too. One year we came second.' But in recent seasons, Arsenal have proved more than a match for anyone. Terry McDermott can no longer get away with his crack that the best two clubs in London are Stringfellow's and The Hippodrome.

LEAGUE CHAMPIONS WHO HAVE PLAYED IN DIVISION FOUR

Burnley
Huddersfield Town
Portsmouth
Preston North End
Sheffield United
Wolverhampton Wanderers

How some of the mighty had fallen. I was particularly sorry to see Burnley sink so low. They're a smashing club and it was great to see them win the Fourth Division championship last season. My association with Burnley goes back to the Sixties when they had wonderful players like Jimmy McIlroy, Jimmy Adamson and Ray Pointer. The thing about Burnley was that they used to pride themselves on producing home-grown players – they're only a relatively small club and couldn't afford the inflated transfer fees of the Tottenhams and Manchester Uniteds. And at the head of Burnley's affairs was their redoubtable chairman Bob Lord, a man who did for diplomacy what Cyril Smith has done for hang-gliding. One of the game's great characters.

TOP 10 FOOTBALL LEAGUE HOTSHOTS (1991-92)

(not including play-offs)

		goals per game
1.	Arsenal	1.92
	Barnet	1.92
3.	Burnley	1.88
4.	Mansfield Town	1.78
5.	Brentford	1.76
	Leeds United	1.76
7.	Blackpool	1.69
8.	Rotherham United	1.66
9.	Stockport County	1.63
10.	Cardiff City	1.57
	Crewe Alexandra	1.57

THE 6 LEAST SUCCESSFUL CURRENT FOOTBALL LEAGUE CLUBS

None of the following have ever won a major trophy:

		Total League games played
1.	Crewe Alexandra	2952
2.	Hartlepool United	2844
3.	Halifax Town	2842
4.	Rochdale	2840
5.	Torquay United	2602
6.	Colchester United	1838

In addition to the above, recent newcomers Scarborough and Barnet have understandably yet to win any major honours although Scarborough, in common with Colchester, have in the past picked up the FA Trophy for non-League clubs. By the same token, Barnet once won the old FA Amateur Cup back in 1946. And the only thing in poor Aldershot's trophy cabinet was cobwebs. Also,

Chester City and Wigan Athletic have so far failed to win any divisional League titles but Chester have had the joy of lifting the Welsh Cup on three occasions while Wigan won the Freight Rover Trophy in 1984-85. Halifax still talk about their glory day. It was in the pre-season Watney Cup for high-scoring teams (a competition, incidentally, won by Colchester in 1972) and Halifax once defeated mighty Manchester United, Best, Law, Charlton and all, in an early round. And woe betide anyone who implies to the good folk of Halifax that maybe United weren't trying that hard!

CURRENT FOOTBALL LEAGUE CLUBS WHO HAVE NEVER PLAYED IN THE TOP TWO DIVISIONS

Barnet
Chester City
Exeter City
Gillingham
Halifax Town
Hartlepool United
Rochdale
Scarborough
Torquay United
Wigan Athletic

Crewe only escape this list by having played in Division Two for four seasons in the 1890 s – but there were only two divisions at the time. Hereford and Mansfield have both managed a solitary season in the old Second while this season is Peterborough's first experience of such exalted status. Curiously, Chester (1936), Exeter (1933), Halifax (1935), Hartlepool (1957), Rochdale (1927) and Torquay (1957) have all been just a place away from promotion to what was Division Two, finishing runners-up in the old regional Third Division when only one club was promoted from each section. Halifax also missed out in the more modern Division Three, coming third behind Preston and Fulham in 1970-71. So near but yet...

THE TOP 30 LEAGUE CLUBS OF THE PAST DECADE

(based on final League placings)

1. Liverpool
2. Arsenal
3. Everton
4. Manchester United
5. Nottingham Forest
6. Tottenham Hotspur
7. Southampton
8. Queen's Park Rangers
9. Aston Villa
10. Norwich City
11. Luton Town
12. Coventry City
13. Sheffield Wednesday
14. West Ham United
15. Chelsea
16. Manchester City
17. Watford
18. Newcastle United
19. Wimbledon
20. Ipswich Town
21. Crystal Palace
22. Leicester City
23. Charlton Athletic
24. Derby County
25. Sunderland
26. Oldham Athletic
27. West Bromwich Albion
28. Blackburn Rovers
29. Portsmouth
30. Oxford United

THE BOTTOM 30 LEAGUE CLUBS OF THE PAST DECADE

(based on final League placings)

1. Halifax Town
2. Rochdale
3. Hereford United
4. Maidstone United
5. Hartlepool United
6. Torquay United
   Wrexham
8. Scarborough
9. Aldershot
10. Colchester United
    Stockport County
12. Crewe Alexandra
13. Barnet
14. Peterborough United
15. Exeter City
16. Northampton Town
17. Darlington
18. Scunthorpe United
19. Burnley
20. Doncaster Rovers
21. Lincoln City
22. York City
23. Chesterfield
24. Tranmere Rovers
25. Mansfield Town
26. Chester City
27. Blackpool
28. Leyton Orient
29. Preston North End
30. Carlisle United
    Southend United

CHAPTER TWO

UP FOR THE CUP

GIANT-KILLERS: THE 15 NON-LEAGUE CLUBS WITH MOST FA CUP VICTORIES OVER LEAGUE TEAMS SINCE 1945

1.	Altrincham	13
2.	Telford United	11
3.	Yeovil Town	10
4.	Wigan Athletic	9
5.	Enfield	8
	Hereford United	8
	Peterborough United	8
8.	Kettering Town	7
	Scarborough	7
10.	Bedford Town	6
	South Shields	6
12.	Bath City	5
	Northwich Victoria	5
14.	Blyth Spartans	4
	Boston United	4
	Gateshead	4
	Leatherhead	4
	Rhyl	4
	Runcorn	4
	Walthamstow Avenue	4
	Weymouth	4

There's nothing quite like the magic of the FA Cup with its David and Goliath battles although as a player, I used to dread being drawn against non-league opposition because you're on a hiding to nothing. I'm glad to say I arrived at Liverpool *after* they had lost 2-1 at Worcester City in 1958-59, in front of 15,000 spectators.

Altrincham's greatest act of giant-killing was when they won 2-1 at First Division Birmingham in 1986, the winning goal coming courtesy of Blues' Robert Hopkins who turned the ball past his own keeper, David Seaman. Ironically, Hopkins had earlier given Birmingham the lead. As I say, it's a great competition although the government did think it was a threat to national security during the First World War. Questions had been raised in the House of Commons after a number of British-made shells had failed to explode in France. It was decided that those making the shells must have been distracted and so no football matches were allowed to take place near munitions factories during working hours. Thus the second Cup replay between Bradford City and Norwich, at Lincoln, was staged behind closed doors.

LEAGUE CLUBS WITH MOST FA CUP DEFEATS AT THE HANDS OF NON-LEAGUE OPPONENTS SINCE 1945

1.	Exeter City	11
	Halifax Town	11
3.	Aldershot	10
	Crewe Alexandra	10
	Stockport County	10
6.	Rochdale	9
7.	Northampton Town	7
8.	Millwall	6
	Torquay United	6
10.	Bournemouth	5
	Colchester United	5
	Lincoln City	5
	Newport County	5
	Oxford United	5
	Southend United	5
	Swansea City	5
	Watford	5

Halifax have gone out to non-league opponents in three years out of the last four – to Kettering, Darlington and Witton Albion. Millwall met a similar fate in four seasons out of eight between 1958-59 and 1965-66. Their greatest humiliation was the 5-2 thumping at Worcester in the round before City disposed of Liverpool. Afterwards the Lions' manager Jimmy Seed tried to excuse the defeat by declaring: 'Our goalkeeper, Reg Davies, was never really tested – except of course for the five goals which passed him.' That's one of the best I've heard yet!

FAMOUS FIRST DIVISION SCALPS

The following are the Non-League teams who have beaten First Division sides in the FA Cup since 1919:

CARDIFF CITY v Oldham Athletic (1919-20)
DARLINGTON v Sheffield Wednesday (1919-20)
CORINTHIANS v Blackburn Rovers (1923-24)
COLCHESTER UNITED v Huddersfield Town (1947-48)
YEOVIL TOWN v Sunderland (1948-49)
HEREFORD UNITED v Newcastle United (1971-72)
WIMBLEDON v Burnley (1974-75)
ALTRINCHAM v Birmingham City (1985-86)
SUTTON UNITED v Coventry City (1988-89)

Yeovil's 2-1 fourth round victory over Sunderland on their famous sloping pitch at The Huish is probably the most celebrated of all Cup slayings. Yeovil's first goal that day was scored by Alec Stock who went on to enjoy tremendous success as a manager, notably with Queen's Park Rangers in the Sixties. But the non-leaguers met their match in the next round. They crashed 8-0 to Manchester United in a game played at Maine Road in front of an incredible crowd of 81,565. When Wimbledon beat Burnley 1-0, they became the first non-league team to beat a Division One side away from home. Ironically, 13 years later when the Dons were winning the Cup itself, Burnley were languishing in the Fourth Division. But my abiding memory of Wimbledon's Cup run back in 1975 was not the

Burnley game but goalkeeper Dickie Guy's penalty save from Peter Lorimer in the Fourth Round clash with mighty Leeds at Elland Road. Lorimer was considered virtually infallible from the spot. He used to blast his penalties and any keeper unfortunate enough to get in the way would probably have ended up in Wakefield. However on this occasion, he tried to place it, but instead presented Guy with a fairly straightforward save. Wimbledon held out for a replay but the dream ended when they went out to a goal deflected in off, of all people, Dave Bassett. Sutton have earned quite a reputation as Cup fighters in recent years. As well as that tremendous win against Coventry, they also held Middlesbrough, then riding high in the Second Division, to a draw at Gander Green Lane in 1988. One of their heroes that day was forward Francis Awaritefe (pronounced our-wa-ra-tee-fee) who proved a handful for defences and referees alike. After Francis was guilty of an over-zealous tackle, the ref reached for his notebook. 'What's your name?' he asked, pen in hand. 'Francis Awaritefe,' came the reply. The baffled ref paused, put away his notebook and said: 'OK. Just don't do it again.'

NON-LEAGUE CLUBS WHO HAVE KNOCKED SECOND DIVISION TEAMS OUT OF THE FA CUP SINCE 1945

COLCHESTER UNITED v Bradford Park Avenue (1947-48)
YEOVIL TOWN v Bury (1948-49)
BISHOP AUCKLAND v Notts County (1954-55)
RHYL v Notts County (1956-57)
PETERBOROUGH UNITED v Lincoln City (1956-57)
WORCESTER CITY v Liverpool (1958-59)
PETERBOROUGH UNITED v Ipswich Town (1959-60)
BLYTH SPARTANS v Stoke City (1977-78)
HARLOW TOWN v Leicester City (1979-80)
WOKING v West Bromwich Albion (1990-91)

NON-LEAGUE CLUBS WHO HAVE REACHED THE LAST 16 OF THE FA CUP SINCE 1919

Cardiff City, 1920 (lost 2-1 to Bristol City)
Plymouth Argyle, 1920 (lost 3-1 to Huddersfield Town)
Colchester United, 1948 (lost 5-0 to Blackpool)
Yeovil Town, 1949 (lost 8-0 to Manchester United)
Blyth Spartans, 1978 (lost 2-1 in a replay to Wrexham)
Telford United, 1985 (lost 3-0 to Everton)

Non-league teams fared considerably better before the First World War with Tottenham Hotspur, then in the Southern League, actually winning the FA Cup in 1901 – the only non-league team ever to do so. They defeated Sheffield United after a replay, the first game at Crystal Palace being watched by what was then a record crowd of 110,820. The Wednesday (1890) and Southampton (1900 and 1902) were losing finalists while the following non-leaguers all reached the semi-finals in those far-off days: Nottingham Forest (1892), Southampton (1898), Millwall (1900 and 1903), and Swindon Town (1910 and 1912). Swindon were yet another team founded by a vicar, the Rev. William Pitt (presumably known in church as Pitt the Elder), who amalgamated a club called Spartans with St Mark's Young Men's Friendly Society. I bet ITV results reader Bob Colston is glad they didn't stick with St Mark's Young Men's Friendly Society!

THE 15 ORIGINAL FA CUP ENTRANTS

Barnes
Civil Service
Clapham Rovers
Crystal Palace (no connection with the present club)
Donington School (Spalding)
Great Marlow
Hampstead Heathens
Harrow Chequers
Hitchin
Maidenhead
Queen's Park
Reigate Priory
Royal Engineers
Upton Park
Wanderers

That first FA Cup in 1871-72, played for a princely little £20 trophy, was won by Wanderers. But it was all rather different from the competition we know today. For a start, Wanderers only had to win one game to reach the final. They received a walk-over in the first round, beat Clapham in the second, went through after only drawing with Crystal Palace in the third and then received another walk-over in the semi-final at the expense of the pride of Glasgow, Queen's Park. The problem was that after drawing the first game, Queen's Park couldn't afford to travel down again for the replay and so Wanderers went on to the final where they overcame the favourites, Royal Engineers, 1-0. The historic winning goal was scored by M.P. Betts, playing under the pseudonym of A.H. Chequer, indicating that he was a member of Harrow Chequers who had scratched to Wanderers in the first round. All very confusing. The biggest disappointment with the final at Kennington Oval was that it was watched by a crowd of only 2,000. The reason for the poor attendance was thought to be the prohibitive entrance fee of 1 s! By the way, the 1878 final between Wanderers and Royal Engineers was refereed by a Mr S.R. Bastard – a great name for a ref.

MOST FA CUP WINS

1.	Tottenham Hotspur	8
2.	Aston Villa	7
	Manchester United	7
4.	Blackburn Rovers	6
	Newcastle United	6
6.	Arsenal	5
	Liverpool	5
	Wanderers	5
	West Bromwich Albion	5
10.	Bolton Wanderers	4
	Everton	4
	Manchester City	4
	Sheffield United	4
	Wolverhampton Wanderers	4
15.	Sheffield Wednesday	3
	West Ham United	3
17.	Bury	2
	Nottingham Forest	2
	Old Etonians	2
	Preston North End	2
	Sunderland	2

G reavsie won two Cup winners' medals with the great Spurs side of the Sixties. The second was when they beat Chelsea in 1967 and Greavsie's partner up front was that wily old fox Alan Gilzean. Like Greavsie, Gilzean was not always one of the world's most enthusiastic trainers. Spurs' coach at the time was 'sergeant major' Eddie Baily who enjoyed nothing more than taking the players on a long road race while he directed operations on a bike. One day, Eddie was having a real go at the tail-enders which needless to say, included Greavsie, Gilzean and also a young Pat Jennings. As they reached the River Lea near Cheshunt, they decided enough was enough. They dragged Eddie off his bike and threw it into the river before showing a rare turn of foot and legging it back to the showers. The last thing Greavsie remembers was Eddie desperately trying to summon help in fishing his bike out of the river.

MOST APPEARANCES IN FA CUP FINALS

1. Arsenal   11
    Everton   11
    Manchester United   11
    Newcastle United   11
5. Liverpool   10
    West Bromwich Albion   10
7. Aston Villa   9
    Tottenham Hotspur   9
9. Blackburn Rovers   8
    Manchester City   8
    Wolverhampton Wanderers   8
12. Bolton Wanderers   7
    Preston North End   7
14. Old Etonians   6
    Sheffield United   6
16. Huddersfield Town   5
    Sheffield Wednesday   5
    The Wanderers   5

One final Arsenal didn't win was the 1927 clash with Cardiff, the only time the FA Cup has gone outside England. The solitary goal was a tragedy for the Gunners' goalkeeper Don Lewis who claimed that a long shot from City's Hugh Ferguson had skidded off his shiny new jersey and into the net. Since that fateful day, Arsenal have insisted on washing and ironing their keepers' jerseys before they are worn. Arsenal also ended up on the losing side against Ipswich in 1978, a match attended by the Rt Hon. Margaret Thatcher, MP, in her capacity as leader of the Conservative party. After the game, keen to show her enthusiasm, she commented: 'I thought the No. 10, Whymark, played exceptionally well'. Unfortunately, although listed in the programme, Trevor Whymark did not actually play!

MOST APPEARANCES IN FA CUP SEMI-FINALS

1.	Everton	22
2.	Liverpool	19
	West Bromwich Albion	19
4.	Manchester United	18
5.	Arsenal	17
	Aston Villa	17
7.	Blackburn Rovers	16
8.	Sheffield Wednesday	15
9	.Derby County	13
	Newcastle United	13
	Tottenham Hotspur	13
	Wolverhampton Wanderers	13

For years it seemed that Derby would never win the Cup – and their perennial misfortune was said to be the result of an old gypsy curse. Their Baseball Ground was built on the site of a gypsy encampment and the dispute which resulted supposedly led to a curse being placed on the club in 1895. True or not, it certainly appeared to work. In 1896 and 1897, they narrowly lost in the semi-finals and the following two years, they were beaten finalists, going down to Nottingham Forest and Sheffield United respectively. Another single-goal semi-final defeat followed in 1902 and when they did reach the final again in 1903, they were overwhelmed 6-0 by Bury. So to 1904 and yet another odd-goal defeat in the semis, this time 1-0 to Bolton. Four semi-finals and three finals in nine years and nothing to show for any of them. The hoodoo lingered on until 1946 when, before the final with Charlton, Derby captain Jack Nicholas asked some gypsies to lift the curse. Suddenly, Derby's luck changed and they won 4-1.

PLAYERS WHO HAVE SCORED IN EVERY ROUND OF THE FA CUP

Sandy Brown (Tottenham Hotspur, 1901)
Ellis Rimmer (Sheffield Wednesday, 1935)
Frank O'Donnell (Preston North End, 1937)
Stan Mortensen (Blackpool, 1948)
Jackie Milburn (Newcastle United, 1951)
Nat Lofthouse (Bolton Wanderers, 1953)
Charlie Wayman (Preston North End, 1954)
Jeff Astle (West Bromwich Albion, 1968)
Peter Osgood (Chelsea, 1970)

Footballers are a superstitious bunch. There are those who insist on wearing the same clothes on match days, others who have strict pre-match rituals and, of course, those who insist on being last out of the dressing-room. It may all sound a load of nonsense but, after hearing the tale of Wednesday winger Ellis Rimmer, I'm not so sure. As he trooped off at half-time in the 1935 final against West Brom, a woman supporter thrust a horseshoe into his hand for good luck. It proved to be a good omen since Rimmer scored twice in the last five minutes to give Wednesday a 4-2 victory. Sandy Brown scored 15 in Spurs' historic Cup run at the start of the century – a record for the competition. The record for most goals in an FA Cup tie proper belongs to that prolific marksman Ted MacDougall who bagged nine in Bournemouth's 11-0 drubbing of Margate in 1971-72 although in a qualifying round in 1947-48, Chris Marron of South Shields had gone one better, scoring ten against Radcliffe Borough. By anyone's standards, that's not bad going.

THE 10 PRESENT LEAGUE CLUBS WITH THE WORST FA CUP RECORDS

(Disregarding recent newcomers Scarborough and Barnet, neither of whom have ever progressed beyond the last 64)

		Appearances in	
		Last 16	Last 32
1.	Hartlepool United	0	3
2.	Torquay United	0	5
3.	Hereford United	0	6
4.	Rochdale	1	1
5.	Tranmere Rovers	1	6
6.	Gillingham	1	8
7.	Halifax Town	2	2
8.	Scunthorpe United	2	6
	Stockport County	2	6
10.	Chester City	2	7
	Darlington	2	7

Hereford may not have enjoyed too much Cup success since joining the League but who could forget Ronnie Radford's rocket which inspired them to that third round victory over First Division Newcastle, Malcolm Macdonald and all, back in 1972? Supermac was never short of confidence, either as a player or as a manager. I love the story about him taking his Huddersfield team to Maine Road for a Second Division fixture in 1987. Huddersfield were playing so well early on that Malcolm turned to his physio and said: 'I think I'll have a cigar – if we keep this up, we'll get double figures.' He was nearly right. The trouble was it was Manchester City who went on to run amok, thrashing Huddersfield 10-1.

CUP FINAL OWN GOALS

Lord Kinnaird (WANDERERS v Oxford University, 1877)
Bert Turner (CHARLTON ATHLETIC v Derby County, 1946)
Mick McGrath (BLACKBURN ROVERS v Wolverhampton
    Wanderers, 1960)
Tommy Hutchison (MANCHESTER CITY v Tottenham
    Hotspur, 1981)
Gary Mabbutt (TOTTENHAM HOTSPUR v Coventry City,
    1987)
Des Walker (NOTTINGHAM FOREST v Tottenham
    Hotspur, 1991)

There are certain things I don't think we'll ever hear from match commentators – like 'A splendid eight-man passing movement there from Cambridge United' or 'And there are thousands locked out at The Shay this afternoon.' Another could well be, 'A deflection off Mabbutt...and just past the post for a corner.' For poor Gary Mabbutt, who almost single-handedly has tried to prop up Spurs' creaky defence in recent years, is one of those unlucky players, off whom deflections nearly always seem to end up in the back of his own net. Strangely Mabbutt, Bert Turner and Tommy Hutchison all scored for both sides when they dropped their Cup final clangers. Charlton's 1946 final with Derby was not only remarkable for Turner's goal for each side and for the lifting of the long-standing Derby curse, but also because the ball burst for the first time in a final. It happened when Derby centre-forward Jackie Stamps fired for goal. It was hard to know which was more deflated, Stamps or the ball, as it wobbled towards Charlton goalkeeper Sam Bartram. And only the previous evening, the referee had confidently stated on the BBC that the odds against that happening were something like a million to one! What's more, when the two clubs met in a League match five days later, the ball burst again. The story doesn't even end there because the following year, Charlton were back at Wembley, against Burnley, and, believe it or not, the ball burst once more. The reason given for these freakish incidents was that immediately after the war, the balls were made of inferior leather.

NON FIRST DIVISION FA CUP WINNERS

Notts County, 1894
Tottenham Hotspur, 1901
Wolverhampton Wanderers, 1908
Barnsley, 1912
West Bromwich Albion, 1931
Sunderland, 1973
Southampton, 1976
West Ham United, 1980

All the above were in the Second Division at the time, except for Spurs, who were members of the Southern League. Spurs' opponents that year were Sheffield United whose goalkeeper was the legendary William 'Fatty' Foulke. At 6ft. 2½ in. tall and weighing 25 stone, Foulke made Dave Beasant look anorexic. He was undoubtedly the heaviest player to appear in the Football League and was capable of punching the ball over the half-way line. He also had a penchant for taking penalties but the story goes that after one unsuccessful spot-kick, he took so long to lumber back to his own goal that the opposition raced upfield and scored in the empty net. As someone who had the pleasure of scoring the winning goal at Wembley in 1965, I know how delighted Trevor Brooking was to score West Ham's winner against Arsenal in 1980 – particularly since Trevor was never renowned for scoring too many with his head. It maybe also went a way to silencing Cloughie's witty but cruel taunt before the match that 'Trevor Brooking floats like a butterfly...and stings like one'.

The symbol of Palace's 1976 Cup run was Malcolm Allison's lucky fedora. The flamboyant Palace manager was never one for letting his teams do the talking and just before Christmas that season, with Palace unbeaten and seven points clear of the field, Big Mal proudly announced that they were the best side ever to grace the Third Division. The record books show otherwise for while Palace reached the semi-finals, they slumped disastrously in the League, to the extent that the one-time racing certainties for the title didn't even manage promotion. They finally finished only fifth. Some observers thought the slump was the result of a curse put on Mal and Palace by hypnotist Romark, others reckoned that all along, Mal had been talking through his hat.

Colchester's appearance in the quarter-finals was the result of their sensational 3-2 victory over Leeds in the fifth round at Layer Road. It was one of the biggest Cup upsets of all time. It was a popular win too in many quarters since Don Revie's Leeds didn't exactly endear themselves to everyone. But they were a great team with players like Johnny Giles, Billy Bremner and that supreme artist, Eddie Gray. I remember Revie once saying of Eddie Gray, 'When he plays on snow, he doesn't leave any footprints.' My old pal the late Willie Ormond, who was Scotland manager, used to rave about Johnny Giles. Willie once said he couldn't understand why Alf Ramsey hadn't picked Giles for England...until it was pointed out that Johnny already had a stack of caps with the Republic of Ireland!

THE 4 LARGEST FA CUP FINAL CROWDS

1. Bolton Wanderers v West Ham United, 1923   126,047
2. Aston Villa v Sunderland, 1913   120,081
3. Tottenham Hotspur v Sheffield United, 1901   110,820
4. Aston Villa v Newcastle United, 1905   101,117

B efore Wembley Stadium was built, the site was a golf course. In fact, there had been plans to erect a giant tower there, a London rival to the Eiffel Tower. But although the foundations for the tower were laid, they began to shift alarmingly and the project was scrapped. A soccer stadium was approved instead and Wembley hosted its first Cup final in 1923 – a match that has gone down in history as the White Horse Final. Fans descended on Wembley from all over the country that day – far more than the stadium could cope with. It is estimated that there were nearly 200,000 people inside, many of them on the pitch, thereby delaying the kick-off for 45 minutes. Helping to clear the masses to the touchlines was policeman G.A. Scorey on his white horse. When play finally started, the crowds were still barely off the pitch. Within two minutes, the ball went out of play and Tresadern, the West Ham left-half, struggling to retrieve it, became entangled in the encircling wall of people and was trapped off the field. While he was out of the action, Bolton scored. They went on to win 2-0. For years afterwards, the Football Association, in appreciation of Mr Scorey's efforts, used to send him complimentary tickets for every Cup final. But each year the FA were bombarded with ticket applications from others claiming that they were the famous policeman on the white horse. Some people will do anything for a free Cup final ticket.

PLAYERS WHO HAVE SCORED IN CONSECUTIVE FA CUP FINALS

Alexander Bonsor (Old Etonians) 1875, 1876
J. Kenrick (Wanderers) 1877, 1878
Lord Kinnaird (Wanderers) 1877 (own goal), 1878
James Forrest (Blackburn Rovers) 1884, 1885
Jimmy Brown (Blackburn Rovers) 1885, 1886
Frederick Dewhurst (Preston North End) 1888, 1889
William Townley (Blackburn Rovers) 1890, 1891
John Southworth (Blackburn Rovers) 1890, 1891
Bobby Johnstone (Manchester City) 1955, 1956
Bobby Smith (Tottenham Hotspur) 1961, 1962

That human battering ram Bobby Smith was a good man to have on your side in a battle. Greavsie told me the story of how burly Bobby influenced the outcome of Spurs' European Cup Winners' Cup tie against the crack Czech team, Slovan Bratislava, in 1962-63. Spurs lost the first leg in Czechoslovakia 2-0 and at the end of the match, the Slovan keeper went up to Bobby to shake his hand. But Bobby refused, merely muttering darkly, 'Londres'. The keeper was mystified but he found out what Bobby meant a fortnight later. After just a few minutes of the return at White Hart Lane, Smithy had softened him up by sending him crashing into the back of the net, ball and all. From then on, the battered keeper didn't want to know. Spurs ended up winning 6-0 on the night and went on to lift the Cup itself, beating Atletico Madrid in the final. There's no way Bobby would get away with those antics these days, not now that goalkeepers are better protected than the Crown Jewels.

CURRENT PREMIER LEAGUE CLUBS WHO HAVE NEVER WON THE FA CUP

Crystal Palace
Middlesbrough
Norwich City
Oldham Athletic
Queen's Park Rangers

Of these, Middlesbrough, Norwich and Oldham have never reached the final. Indeed, Middlesbrough have never got beyond the sixth round while Oldham manager Joe Royle once joked: 'A third round replay would be a Cup run for us.'

EASY PASSAGES TO THE FINAL

The following only had to meet one First Division side en route to winning the FA Cup:

Newcastle United, 1910
Bolton Wanderers, 1926
Liverpool, 1992

The way Liverpool struggled against Bristol Rovers, Ipswich and Portsmouth last season, you certainly wouldn't say that their path to glory turned out to be easy, but the fact remains that they did only have to face one First Division outfit, Aston Villa. At the other end of the scale, three clubs have encountered all-First Division opposition on their way to lifting the Cup – Sheffield United (1899), Bury (1903) and Manchester United (1948).

SECOND DIVISION BEATEN FINALISTS IN THE FA CUP

Bolton Wanderers, 1904
Barnsley, 1910
Huddersfield Town, 1920
Wolverhampton Wanderers, 1921
West Ham United, 1923
Sheffield United, 1936
Burnley, 1947
Leicester City, 1949
Preston North End, 1964
Fulham, 1975
Queen's Park Rangers, 1982
Sunderland, 1992

Wolves may have lost 1-0 to Spurs in 1921 but 13 years earlier they had lifted the Cup, beating Newcastle 3-1. And one of their scorers that day was a vicar! The Rev. Kenneth Hunt scored their first goal against the Magpies and thus became the only clergyman to collect an FA Cup winners' medal. He was also the last amateur to do so. Rumour has it that when he told his team-mates that God was on their side, the ref demanded to know why his name wasn't on the team-sheet.

RELEGATED FA CUP FINALISTS

Manchester City, 1926
Leicester City, 1969
Brighton & Hove Albion, 1983

A good Cup run can often have an adverse effect on League form, as these three clubs found to their cost. To add insult to injury, all three lost in the final. Brighton were particularly unlucky, only going down in a replay to Manchester United. And but for a glaring last-minute miss by Gordon Smith in the first match, when he shot straight at United keeper Gary Bailey from ten yards, Brighton would have won. Smith's nightmare is still remembered on the South Coast and is immortalised in the Seagulls' fanzine, titled *And Smith Must Score!*

FA CUP FINALS THAT HAVE GONE TO EXTRA TIME

Royal Engineers v Old Etonians 1875*
Wanderers v Oxford University 1877
Blackburn Olympic v Old Etonians 1883
Barnsley v West Bromwich Albion 1912*
Aston Villa v Huddersfield Town 1920
Preston North End v Huddersfield Town 1938
Derby County v Charlton Athletic 1946
Charlton Athletic v Burnley 1947
Liverpool v Leeds United 1965
West Bromwich Albion v Everton 1968
Chelsea v Leeds United 1970*
Arsenal v Liverpool 1971
Tottenham Hotspur v Manchester City 1981*
Tottenham Hotspur v Queen's Park Rangers 1982*
Manchester United v Brighton 1983*
Manchester United v Everton 1985
Coventry City v Tottenham Hotspur 1987
Liverpool v Everton 1989
Manchester United v Crystal Palace 1990*
Tottenham Hotspur v Nottingham Forest 1991

In addition, six other finals went to replays without extra time in the first game – Wanderers v Old Etonians (1876), Blackburn Rovers v West Brom (1886), Spurs v Sheffield United (1901), Sheffield United v Southampton (1902), Newcastle v Barnsley (1910) and Bradford City v Newcastle (1911). The closest contest of all must be Chelsea v

* Denotes replay necessary.

Leeds in 1970 where both the first encounter and the replay went to extra time before David Webb bundled in that dramatic winner.

CLUBS WITH MOST FA CUP TIE VICTORIES OVER THE PAST 10 YEARS

1.	Liverpool	36
2.	Everton	31
3.	Manchester United	29
4.	Sheffield Wednesday	21
	Watford	21
6.	West Ham United	20
7.	Norwich City	19
	Wigan Athletic	19
9.	Arsenal	18
	Southampton	18
	Tottenham Hotspur	18
12.	Blackpool	17
	Brighton & Hove Albion	17
	Nottingham Forest	17
15.	Bournemouth	16
	Sheffield United	16
	Wimbledon	16
18.	Bristol City	15
	Cambridge United	15
	Notts County	15
21.	Bolton Wanderers	14
	Brentford	14
	Burnley	14
	Reading	14
	Scunthorpe United	14
	Swindon Town	14
	Walsall	14

Watford's trip to Wembley in 1984 was particularly poignant for chairman Elton John, the man who liked the club so much he bought it. Twenty-five years earlier, he had stood heartbroken on the Wembley terraces as his uncle, Roy Dwight, was carried off with a broken leg after opening the scoring for Nottingham Forest in their 2-1 victory over Luton. Alas, there were no happy returns for Elton who this time sat in the Royal box – Watford lost 2-0 to Everton. Elton did wonders for Watford and, although he was obviously disappointed not to win the Cup, he didn't let it get him down. To prove the point, even though a lot of people blamed Watford keeper Steve Sherwood for allowing Andy Gray to bundle the ball into the net for Everton's second goal, and Steve subsequently moved on to Grimsby, he and Elton still exchange Christmas cards. Mind you, I don't know what the message inside says...

CLUBS WITH FEWEST FA CUP TIE VICTORIES OVER THE PAST 10 YEARS

1.	Bury	3
	Leicester City	3
	Southend United	3
	Stockport County	3
	Wolverhampton Wanderers	3
6.	Chesterfield	4
	Lincoln City	4
8.	Carlisle United	5
	Charlton Athletic	5
	Fulham	5
	Stoke City	5

Stoke have always been unlucky in the Cup, dating right back to the 1890 s. During a quarter-final tie with Notts County in 1890-1, a Stoke shot was punched off the line by the County left-back with the goalkeeper well beaten. However, in those days there was no such thing as a penalty so instead Stoke had to take a free-kick on the goal-line which the keeper saved easily. County won 1-0 but the incident created such controversy that the FA decided to introduce penalties from September 1891. Not that it helped Stoke much for shortly after the new rule was adopted, they were trailing 1-0 at Aston Villa in a League match when they were awarded a penalty two minutes from time. The Villa keeper promptly picked up the ball and booted it out of the ground. By the time it had been found, the ref had blown for full-time! Needless to say, after that, the rule was amended to allow time to be added on for taking a penalty.

MOST FA YOUTH CUP FINAL APPEARANCES

1.	Manchester United	9
2.	Everton	5
	West Ham United	5
	Wolverhampton Wanderers	5
5.	Arsenal	4
	Manchester City	4
7.	Aston Villa	3
	Chelsea	3
	Coventry City	3
	Crystal Palace	3
	Watford	3
	West Bromwich Albion	3

Manchester United lead the way with seven wins, including the first five tournaments from 1953-57. Of course, those were the days of the fabulous Busby Babes and the 1956 final against Chesterfield saw United's Bobby Charlton score past a young keeper by the name of Gordon Banks. The most remarkable final was the 1958 clash between Wolves and Chelsea. Wolves were 5-1 down after the first leg but won 6-1 at Molineux to take the Cup 7-6 on aggregate. Three clubs have lifted the FA Cup and the FA Youth Cup in the same year – Arsenal (1971), Everton (1984) and Coventry (1987). Coventry had twice previously been losing finalists, the second time to Spurs in 1970. Their goalkeeper in that final was former BBC frontman turned 'Son of God', David Icke. No divine intervention then though as Spurs took the Cup 4-3 on aggregate, the winning goal being scored by a young Graeme Souness.

CHAPTER THREE

SCOTTISH SCENE

MOST SUCCESSFUL SCOTTISH CLUBS IN HISTORY

(including League, Cup, League Cup and European competitions)

		Trophies won
1.	Rangers	84
2.	Celtic	74
3.	Aberdeen	17
4.	Heart of Midlothian	13
5.	Queen's Park	10
6.	Hibernian	8
7.	Dundee	5
8.	East Fife	4
	Motherwell	4

The table shows how the two Glasgow giants have dominated Scottish football. And Rangers might have added another one to their total had they not displayed a fit of pique back in 1879. In the Scottish Cup final that year, Rangers drew 1-1 with Vale of Leven but were adamant that they had a perfectly good second goal disallowed. They protested to the Scottish FA but their pleas fell on deaf ears. So Rangers sulked and refused to turn up for the replay. Thus Vale of Leven kicked off, ran the ball through the unguarded goal and were declared the winners! It must have looked like something out of that classic Monty Python sketch where the Bournemouth Gynaecologists played the Watford Long John Silver Impersonators.

THE 10 OLDEST CURRENT SCOTTISH LEAGUE CLUBS

1.	Queen's Park	1867
2.	Kilmarnock	1869
3.	Stranraer	1870
4.	Dumbarton	1872
5.	Rangers	1873
6.	Heart of Midlothian	1874
	Morton	1874
8.	Hamilton Academicals	1875
	Hibernian	1875
10.	Falkirk	1876
	Partick Thistle	1876

The origins of organised football in Scotland lay with young men from the north of the country who flocked to Glasgow in the 1860s. They banded together to indulge in typical Highland sports such as caber-tossing and hammer-throwing on an open piece of ground in Pollokshields but when that site was required for building, the youngsters moved on to Queen's Park Recreation Ground. There they spotted a group of lads from the YMCA kicking a ball about in a 20-a-side game and quickly realised that this new game was more fun than tossing the caber. They got together and formed The Queen's Park Foot Ball Club. The trouble was being the only football club in Scotland, they had to play amongst themselves. So if 80 of their members turned up on a Saturday afternoon, the game would be 40-a-side. Nor were there any rules as such – even a rugby touch-down was permitted. Indeed one of their first match reports in 1869 stated that Queen's Park 'were the winners by four goals and nine touches down'. It really was a funny old game.

THE 10 YOUNGEST CURRENT SCOTTISH LEAGUE CLUBS

1.	Meadowbank Thistle	1974
2.	Clydebank	1965
3.	Stirling Albion	1945
4.	Queen of the South	1919
5.	Ayr United	1910
6.	Dundee United (as Dundee Hibs)	1909
7.	Brechin City	1906
8.	Aberdeen	1903
	East Fife	1903
10.	Dundee	1893

Meadowbank's election to the League caused a real furore. As works team Ferranti Thistle, they had been going since 1943 and had graduated from playing on public parks to a home at City Park, the former home of one-time Scottish League members Edinburgh City. But Thistle enjoyed only moderate success, nothing to equal the achievements of many of the Highland League clubs. So when they were elected in preference to the likes of Elgin or one of the Inverness teams, there was widespread disbelief. Of course, the deciding factor was geographical – not many clubs fancied long trips to the Highlands. The two provisos on Thistle joining the League were that they changed their name and found a better ground. When Edinburgh City Council allowed the club to use the newly-built Meadowbank Stadium, both criteria were met. Although the Stadium holds 16,500, it cannot cope with the segregation needed for big Cup ties so these take place either at Tynecastle, the home of Hearts, or at Hibs' ground, Easter Road. And for ordinary League matches, only the main stand, holding 7,500, is used. Alas, sometimes Thistle's gates are so small that the press box would almost suffice.

FOUNDER MEMBERS OF THE SCOTTISH LEAGUE

Abercorn
Celtic
Cowlairs
Cambuslang
Dumbarton
Heart of Midlothian
Rangers
Renton
St Mirren
Third Lanark
Vale of Leven

The Scottish League was founded in 1890 and, on the surface at least, was strictly amateur. But clubs secretly had to pay their best players to prevent them defecting to England and finally in 1893-94, professionalism arrived officially. However this was not before the Scottish FA had ensured that powerful Western club Renton, one of the favourites for the title, only lasted five matches of that inaugural League season. The SFA had suspended the Edinburgh club St Bernard's for paying a player. Suddenly a new team appeared calling themselves Edinburgh Saints and Renton played them in a friendly. The SFA decreed Edinburgh Saints and St Bernard's to be one and the same and as a result Renton were expelled from the Association. This meant they couldn't play in the League either and so they were kicked out. But Renton were allowed to return the following season. The first League title was actually shared by Rangers and Dumbarton. They tied on points (Dumbarton would have won comfortably had goal difference or average been in effect), drew 2-2 in a play-off and were declared joint champions.

MOST SCOTTISH LEAGUE
CHAMPIONSHIPS

1.	Rangers	42
2.	Celtic	35
3.	Aberdeen	4
	Heart of Midlothian	4
	Hibernian	4
6.	Dumbarton	2
7.	Dundee	1
	Dundee United	1
	Kilmarnock	1
	Motherwell	1
	Third Lanark	1

Rangers' most prolific period was the 1920s and 1930s when they won the title on no fewer than 14 occasions including five years in a row between 1927 and 1931. In fact, in the season 1929-30, the club won every competition it entered – the Scottish League, the Scottish Cup, the Reserve Cup, the Reserve Championship, the Glasgow Cup and the Glasgow Charity Cup. They would probably have won the Scottish Grand National too! Their driving force was manager William Struth who took over in 1920 after his predecessor William Wilton had drowned. Struth liked to be as smart off the field as his team were on it, and always used to keep half a dozen double-breasted suits in his office. It was nothing for him to change two or three times a day. He made Ron Atkinson look like Rab C. Nesbitt.

SCOTTISH CLUBS WITH MOST DIVISIONAL TITLES

(not including the overall League championship)

1.	Ayr United	7
	Clyde	7
	Stirling Albion	7
4.	Morton	6
5	Falkirk	5
	St Johnstone	5
7.	Hibernian	4
	Leith Athletic	4
	Motherwell	4
	Partick Thistle	4
	Raith Rovers	4

Of the current League clubs, only Arbroath, Stenhousemuir and Stranraer have failed to win a divisional title although it's been years since Alloa Athletic brought home any silverware. They topped Division Two back in 1921-22, their very first season in the League, and in the process became the first Scottish club to be promoted, the previous method of election to Division One having been scrapped. Stirling Albion's success is definitely worth a mention since they only joined the League in 1948. From 1921 to 1939, Stirling's League side had been King's Park but their Forthbank Park ground was badly damaged in 1940 by the only bomb dropped on the town during the war, from a lone German plane which, it would appear, decided to fire its missile at random. Reflecting on his bad luck and amidst considerable controversy, coal merchant Tom Fergusson, the former chairman of King's Park, decided not to resurrect the club. There were rumours that he was involved in a bribery scandal at Forthbank. Instead he arranged the purchase of the Annfield estate for £5,000 and created a new club, Stirling Albion. The club derived its name from the Albion trucks which formed makeshift stands in the early days at Annfield. There were no proper stands and so club officials had to watch the game perched on chairs in the back of these freshly-cleaned trucks.

Somehow I don't think Shanks would have stood for that at the other Anfield...

MOST RELEGATED SCOTTISH LEAGUE CLUBS

1.	Clyde	10
2.	Morton	9
3.	Dunfermline Athletic	8
4.	Falkirk	7
	Raith Rovers	7
	Stirling Albion	7
7.	Kilmarnock	6
	Queen of the South	6

CLUBS WHO HAVE SUPPLIED MOST FULL SCOTTISH INTERNATIONALS

1.	Rangers	122
2.	Celtic	102
3.	Queen's Park	75
4.	Heart of Midlothian	61
5.	Hibernian	49
6.	Aberdeen	41
7.	Dundee	34
8.	Newcastle United	25
9.	Kilmarnock	24
10.	Everton	22

I was fortunate enough to play in the same Scotland side as greats like Denis Law, Dave Mackay, Willie Henderson, Jim Baxter, Pat Crerand and the late John White. Wee Willie was a real character. I remember the time when a national newspaper picked him out as being one of the ten ugliest men in Scotland. Willie was livid and his mood was not helped by a girl who accosted him in the street that very day. 'Excuse me,' she said. 'Are you Willie Henderson?' His ego bruised by the article, Willie insisted that he wasn't, but the girl kept pestering him as he walked on. Eventually, he turned and snapped: 'Look, I've told you twice already. I'm not Willie Henderson – now get lost.' To which the girl replied: 'Well, I'll tell you something…you're just as ——ing ugly!'

CURRENT SCOTTISH LEAGUE CLUBS WHO HAVE NEVER SUPPLIED A FULL INTERNATIONAL

Berwick Rangers
Brechin City
Clydebank
Forfar Athletic
Meadowbank Thistle
Stenhousemuir
Stirling Albion
Stranraer

It's a minor miracle that some of these towns can support a League club let alone ever contemplate producing an international. With a population of around 6,500, Brechin is little more than a large village and is the smallest place in Britain to boast a League team. Their quaint home, Glebe Park, is also the only League ground in Britain to have a thick hedge growing along one touchline. Can you imagine Arsenal replacing the North Bank with a row of privet bushes?

CLUBS WITH MOST SCOTTISH LEAGUE GOALS IN HISTORY

1.	Rangers	7185
2.	Celtic	6964
3.	Heart of Midlothian	5854
4.	Airdrieonians	5415
5.	Motherwell	5376
6.	Morton	5318
7.	Hibernian	5276
8.	Dundee	5126
9.	Kilmarnock	5032
10.	Clyde	5025

I was thrilled to play for Motherwell, even though I only earned £16 a week in 1960 as a part-timer. We had a fair side but when I heard that Newcastle United were keen to sign me, I wanted the chance to move on. I asked for a transfer and Motherwell granted my request on the evening we were playing Hamilton in a Lanarkshire Cup tie. I scored a hat-trick but as I was about to set off for home after the match, Motherwell manager Bobby Ancell said: 'Sit where you are – there's a club here to talk to you.' In walked Bill Shankly, dressed like James Cagney, and about to make me an offer I couldn't refuse. 'How would you like to come to Liverpool? We're going to be the greatest team in the country. We've the greatest supporters, we've the greatest training ground. You come to us.' I was so mesmerised by the man that I never even asked what Liverpool were going to pay me. When I did get home that night, Newcastle boss Charlie Mitten was waiting, but one meeting with Shanks had just about convinced me. And so I signed for Liverpool on £30 a week.

CLUBS WITH MOST SCOTTISH LEAGUE GOALS SCORED IN A SEASON

1.	Raith Rovers (1937-38, D2)	142
2.	Morton (1963-64, D2)	135
3.	Falkirk (1935-36, D2)	132
	Heart of Midlothian (1957-58, D1)	132
5.	Ayr United (1936-37, D2)	122
	Clyde (1956-57, D2)	122
7.	Cowdenbeath (1938-39, D2)	120
	Dunfermline Athletic (1957-58, D2)	120
9.	Motherwell (1931-32, D1)	119
10.	Rangers (1931-32, D1)	118
	Rangers (1933-34, D1)	118

CLUBS WITH MOST SCOTTISH LEAGUE GOALS CONCEDED IN A SEASON

1.	Edinburgh City (1931-32, D2)	146
2.	Brechin City (1937-38, D2)	139
3.	Forfar Athletic (1938-39, D2)	138
4.	Leith (1931-32, D1)	137
5.	Edinburgh City (1937-38, D2)	135
6.	Edinburgh City (1934-35, D2)	134
7.	Edinburgh City (1932-33, D2)	133
	Montrose (1955-56, Division B)	133
9.	East Stirlingshire (1938-39, D2)	130
10.	Morton (1937-38, D1)	127

Edinburgh City were definitely the team to practise your shooting on in the 1930s. They let in a staggering 981 League goals in eight seasons. No wonder they decided to call it a day shortly after the War – their keeper must have had chronic backache from picking the ball out of the net. The dubious honour for the most miserable season belongs either to Vale of Leven who failed to win any of their 22 games in 1891-92, picking up just five points, or more recently, Forfar, who in 1974-75, won only one out of 38 Second Division fixtures and ended up with a grand total of nine points. Yet within three years, under the guidance of Archie Knox who later assisted Alex Ferguson at Old Trafford, Forfar had emerged from that nightmare season to get within seven minutes of a first-ever place in the Scottish League Cup final. They led mighty Rangers 2-1 but then the Glasgow giants scored an 83 rd minute equaliser and went on to win 5-2 in extra time. The 1990-91 season was pretty dismal for Hibernian who failed to win away in the League. One supporter voiced his discontent by noting: 'Hibs have 66 players on their books – that's a team for every day of the week except Saturday.'

FORMER CLUB NAMES

Excelsior FC (Airdrieonians)
Dundee Hibernian (Dundee United)
Bainsford Britannia (East Stirlingshire)
Ferranti Thistle (Meadowbank Thistle)

Whatever else you may say about Scottish football, you have to admit that the clubs have some splendid names. Somehow Hamilton Academicals against Queen of the South has a real romantic ring about it. The Accies were so called because they originated from Hamilton Academy while Queen of the South is a title often bestowed on the club's home town of Dumfries. Morton took their name from Morton Terrace in Greenock where many of their early players lived, Raith Rovers play in Kirkcaldy but were named after the Laird of Raith and Novar while the grandiose Heart of Midlothian was inspired by a famous old Edinburgh dance club. I can't see Joe Jordan doing the military two-step...

THE LAST 8 CLUBS TO JOIN THE SCOTTISH LEAGUE

1. Meadowbank Thistle   1974
2. Clydebank   1966
3. Stranraer   1955
4. Berwick Rangers   1951
5. Stirling Albion   1947
6. Edinburgh City   1930
7. Montrose   1929
8. Queen of the South   1925

A team under the name of Clydebank were members of the Scottish League between 1914 and 1931 but they were no relation to the present club. The new Clydebank first joined the League in the Sixties as part of an acrimonious 12-month merger with East Stirlingshire. East Stirling's floodlights and some roofing were shifted to Clydebank's home at New Kilbowie Park and a club played in the League as E.S. Clydebank which sounds like a good pen name for a Scottish thriller writer. But after a court case brought against them by East Stirling, the two clubs resumed their separate identities and, after a season back in junior football, Clydebank entered the League in their own right in 1966. Like so many of the smaller clubs, Montrose have always had to count the pennies. In their early days, they had to borrow goalnets from a local junior club and had to buy a second-hand stand from the Montrose Highland Games. And when they joined the League, they encountered another problem – chickens were wandering into the ground and damaging the pitch. Surely the first professional fowl...

THE LAST 20 CLUBS TO LEAVE THE SCOTTISH LEAGUE

1.	Third Lanark	1967
2.	Leith Athletic	1953
3.	Edinburgh City	1949
4.	King's Park	1939
	St Bernard's	1939
6.	Armadale	1932
	Bo'ness	1932
8.	Clydebank	1931
9.	Arthurlie	1929
10.	Bathgate	1928
11.	Nithsdale Wanderers	1927
12.	Beith	1926
	Broxburn United	1926
	Dykehead	1926
	Helensburgh	1926
	Johnstone	1926
	Lochgelly United	1926
	Mid-Annandale	1926
	Peebles Rovers	1926
	Royal Albert	1926
	Solway Star	1926
	Vale of Leven	1926

The reason for the mass exodus in 1926 was the demise of the short-lived Third Division of the Scottish League. Meanwhile Armadale and Bo'ness were both expelled in 1932 for failing to meet gate money guarantees to their opponents.

THE TOP 15 SCOTTISH LEAGUE CLUBS
OVER THE PAST DECADE

(Based on final League positions)

1. Celtic
2. Rangers
3. Aberdeen
4. Dundee United
5. Heart of Midlothian
6. Hibernian
7. St Mirren
8. Dundee
9. Motherwell
10. Falkirk
11. Clydebank
12. Hamilton Academicals
13. Morton
14. Airdrieonians
15. Partick Thistle

It's great to see Partick Thistle back in the big time this season. They haven't had much to shout about since they shook Celtic 4-1 in that great League Cup final upset back in 1972. For so long, they've been one of the Cinderella teams of Glasgow, the butt of countless jokes. Billy Connolly says that for years he thought the club's name was Partick Thistle Nil!

THE BOTTOM 15 SCOTTISH LEAGUE CLUBS OVER THE PAST DECADE

(Based on final League positions)

1. East Stirlingshire
2. Stranraer
3. Berwick Rangers
4. Arbroath
5. Albion Rovers
6. Stenhousemuir
7. Cowdenbeath
8. Queen's Park
9. Montrose
10. Queen of the South
11. Stirling Albion
12. Alloa Athletic
13. East Fife
14. Brechin City
15. Ayr United

I know things have been tough for Queen of the South but last season their manager Ally MacLeod (yes, *the* Ally MacLeod) turned out for their reserves at the ripe old age of 58! What's more, he even scored from the penalty spot against St Mirren although the fairytale didn't have a happy ending – Queens lost 8-1. There's no truth in the rumour that Ally's trying to set the record straight after Argentina in 1978 by fighting his way into the 1994 World Cup reckoning as a player.

MOST SCOTTISH LEAGUE CUP WINS

1.	Rangers	17
2.	Celtic	9
3.	Aberdeen	4
	Heart of Midlothian	4
5.	Dundee	3
	East Fife	3

East Fife are unique in Scottish football. They are the only Second Division club to win the Scottish Cup (they beat Kilmarnock 4-2 in a replay in 1938) and are similarly the only Division Two team to lift the League Cup. Their trio of successes, achieved at the expense of Falkirk, Dunfermline and Partick respectively, occurred between 1948 and 1954, the victory over Dunfermline in 1950 being masterminded by manager Scot Symon who went on to even greater things as boss of Rangers. A measure of the little Methil club's achievement is that, apart from Raith Rovers in 1948-49, Dunfermline in 1949-50, Kilmarnock in 1952-53, Morton in 1963-64 and Dundee in 1980-81, no other club from outside the top flight has even reached the final of the League Cup. When they achieved their historic Scottish Cup triumph against Kilmarnock, East Fife were so short of players that they had to sign Danny McKerrall from Falkirk Reserves just for the game. This was because their regular outside-left was injured and they had nobody to play in that position. Not only was McKerrall's only Scottish Cup tie a final but he collected a winners' medal and scored two crucial goals into the bargain!

HAT-TRICK HEROES IN SCOTTISH LEAGUE CUP FINALS

Davie Duncan (East Fife) v Falkirk, 1947-48
Willie Bauld (Heart of Midlothian) v Motherwell, 1954-55
John Mc Phail (Celtic) v Rangers, 1957-58

Jim Forrest (4 goals) (Rangers) v Morton, 1963-64
Bobby Lennox (Celtic) v Hibernian, 1968-69
Dixie Deans (Celtic) v Hibernian, 1974-75
Joe Harper (Hibernian) v Celtic, 1974-75
Ally Mc Coist (Rangers) v Celtic, 1983-84

You have to feel sorry for Hibs' Joe Harper. He scored a hat-trick in the final but still ended up with a losers' medal as Celtic romped home 6-3. Between 1964 and 1978, Celtic appeared in no fewer than 14 consecutive League Cup finals of which they won only six. But they ended a run of four successive defeats when they hammered Hibs. One of the stars of the show that day was winger Jimmy Johnstone, one of the all-time great crowd-pleasers. When Tommy Docherty was appointed Scotland manager, he joked that on his first day he had to call off training after half-an-hour because nobody could get the ball off wee Jimmy.

MOST SCOTTISH FA CUP WINS

1.	Celtic	29
2.	Rangers	25
3.	Queen's Park	10
4.	Aberdeen	7
5.	Heart of Midlothian	5
6.	Clyde	3
	St Mirren	3
	Vale of Leven	3

Probably the most famous Scottish Cup tie of all was Arbroath's record 36-0 trouncing of Bon Accord in 1885. It was all a ghastly mistake really because the Scottish FA sent the invitation to Orion Cricket Club instead of Orion FC from Aberdeen. But the cricketers decided to have a go anyway, changed their name to Bon Accord and the rest, as they say, is history. It was all so one-sided that reports stated that the Arbroath goalkeeper spent most of the match smoking his pipe while sheltering from the rain under an umbrella.

CLUBS WITH MOST SCOTTISH FA CUP FINAL APPEARANCES

1.	Celtic	46
2.	Rangers	41
3.	Aberdeen	13
4.	Queen's Park	12
5.	Heart of Midlothian	10
	Hibernian	10
7.	Kilmarnock	7
	Vale of Leven	7
9.	Clyde	6
	Dumbarton	6
	Dundee United	6
	Motherwell	6
	St Mirren	6
	Third Lanark	6
15.	Renton	5
16.	Dundee	4
17.	Airdrieonians	3
	Dunfermline Athletic	3
	East Fife	3

All-conquering pioneers Queen's Park had been in existence nearly nine years before they so much as conceded a goal! Vale of Leven scored against them in the 1875-76 Cup semi-final but still went under 3-1. But on 30 December 1876, the unthinkable happened. Queen's Park lost their first game in Scotland, a fifth-round Cup tie, 2-1 to...Vale of Leven.

CLUBS WITH MOST SCOTTISH FA CUP SEMI-FINAL APPEARANCES

1.	Celtic	58
2.	Rangers	51
3.	Aberdeen	27
4.	Heart of Midlothian	25
5.	Hibernian	23
6.	Third Lanark	18
7.	Motherwell	17
	Queen's Park	17
	St Mirren	17
10.	Dundee	16

Celtic only came into existence in 1888 but amazingly by February the following year, they were appearing in their first Scottish Cup final – against Third Lanark at the Hi Hi's old home, Cathkin Park. But for Celtic, it wasn't a particularly happy introduction to the vagaries of senior football. A morning blizzard left a covering of snow on the pitch but SFA officials passed it fit for play. Then as the crowds poured in, there was a further snowstorm. The SFA admitted that the pitch was unplayable but still ordered the match to proceed. Both teams protested but to no avail. However, the players were said to be under the impression that it was nothing more than a friendly and that the Cup wasn't at stake. Third Lanark defied the conditions to win 3-0 and then, to Celtic's amazement, promptly claimed the Cup, denying that they had ever agreed to play a friendly. Understandably, Celtic were not amused. The SFA stepped into the fray and ordered a replay which Third Lanark won 2-1. It just shows that gamesmanship isn't a modern invention.

10 SCOTTISH FA CUP GIANT-KILLING ACTS

Bathgate 1, Falkirk 0 (round 2, 1922)
Bo'ness 3, Hearts 2 (round 2, 1923)
Duns 2, Dumbarton 0 (round 2, 1937)
East Fife 2, Aberdeen 1 (round 3, 1938)
Berwick Rangers 3, Dundee 0 (round 3, 1954)
Ayr United 2, Inverness Caledonian 4 (round 5, 1955)
Fraserburgh 1, Dundee 0 (round 1, 1959)
Berwick Rangers 1, Rangers 0 (round 2, 1967)
Elgin City 2, Ayr United 0 (round 1, 1967)
Hamilton Academicals 2, Keith 3 (round 3, 1980)

Far and away the biggest shock in the history of the Scottish Cup was Berwick's 1-0 victory over Rangers. To add to Rangers' humiliation, Berwick are, of course, based in England. The only goal of the game was scored by Sammy Reid but the man who kept Rangers at bay was Berwick keeper Jock Wallace who later went on to become a no-nonsense manager at Ibrox. The only non-League sides to reach the quarter-finals in modern times are Eyemouth United in 1960 (they lost 2-1 to Kilmarnock) and Elgin City in 1968. They went down 2-1 at Morton.

THE ORIGINAL 16 ENTRANTS FOR THE SCOTTISH FA CUP

Alexandria Athletic
Blytheswood
Callander
Clydesdale
Dumbarton
Dumbreck
Eastern
Granville
Kilmarnock
Queen's Park
Renton
Rovers
Southern
Third Lanark
Vale of Leven
Western

The very first Scottish FA Cup tie took place in October 1873, with Kilmarnock meeting Renton at Crosshill which was then the home of Queen's Park. Unfortunately, Kilmarnock were more accustomed to playing rugby and the *Glasgow Evening News* reported at the time that the team was not 'thoroughly conversant with Association rules. On account of this, the Renton club kept the ball well up to the goal posts of their opponents as they received several free-kicks in succession thro' some of the Auld Killie's men persistently using their hands.' Hardly surprisingly, Killie lost 3-0 – and they were a man short. There were numerous protests in the early days. The best one was by Rangers, after going down 4-3 at Arbroath in 1884. They complained that the pitch wasn't wide enough and indeed when it was measured, it was discovered to be 35 inches short. It clearly made a big difference to the Rangers players for when the game was replayed five weeks later, they duly won 8-0. Who says size isn't everything?

PLAYERS WHO HAVE WON 7 SCOTTISH FA CUP WINNERS' MEDALS

Jimmy McMenemy (6 with Celtic (1904, 1907, 1908, 1911, 1912, 1914), 1 with Partick Thistle (1921))
Bob McPhail (1 with Airdrieonians (1924), 6 with Rangers (1928, 1930, 1932, 1934, 1935, 1936))
Billy McNeill (all with Celtic (1965, 1967, 1969, 1971, 1972, 1974, 1975))

As Greavsie never tires of reminding me, I had the misfortune to play against him when Scotland were beaten 9-3 by England in that famous 1960 international at Wembley. The result launched a thousand English wise-cracks, the most repeated of course being, 'What's the time?' 'Nearly ten past Haffey', in memory of the hapless Scottish goalkeeper Frank Haffey. Along with many of my country-men, I thought poor Frank was wrongly pilloried afterwards – he didn't have much chance with most of the goals that went past him. Billy McNeill was in the Scotland side too that day and the joke in the Scottish camp afterwards (we didn't lose our sense of humour entirely) was that our defence had crumbled because the match was played with an orange ball. Rangers' Protestant full-backs Eric Caldow and Bobby Shearer had been afraid to kick it and Catholic Billy McNeill was afraid to touch it!

CURRENT LEAGUE CLUBS WITH THE WORST RECORD IN THE SCOTTISH FA CUP

		Appearances in	
		Last 8	Last 16
1.	Stranraer	0	4
2.	Brechin City	0	6
3.	Meadowbank Thistle	0	8
4.	Cowdenbeath	1	12
5.	Berwick Rangers	2	3
6.	East Stirlingshire	2	11
7.	Alloa Athletic	3	8
8.	Montrose	4	4
9.	Stirling Albion	6	9

With a best-ever League season of fourth in the Second Division and never having reached the quarter-finals of the Cup, little Stranraer are the least successful of the current clubs. But they can take consolation from the fact that they've done a lot better than Glasgow team Thistle. They joined the League in 1893-94 and finished bottom of the Second Division with just two victories. Perhaps not surprisingly, they decided that dismal first season would be their last – and quit. Following on from this list, six of the current League clubs have reached the semi-finals on only one occasion – Arbroath (1947), Ayr United (1973), Clydebank (1990), Forfar Athletic (1982), Queen of the South (1950) and Stenhousemuir way back in 1903.

THE 20 LARGEST SCOTTISH FA CUP FINAL ATTENDANCES

1. Celtic v Aberdeen, 1937   147,365
2. Motherwell v Dundee, 1952   136,274
3. Heart of Midlothian v Celtic, 1956   133,339
4. Celtic v Rangers, 1969   132,847
5. Rangers v Morton, 1948 (replay)   131,975
6. Celtic v Motherwell, 1951   131,943
7. Celtic v Aberdeen, 1954   129,926
8. Rangers v Aberdeen, 1953   129,681
9. Rangers v Celtic, 1963   129,527
10. Rangers v Morton, 1948   129,176
11. Celtic v Aberdeen, 1967   127,117
12. Rangers v St Mirren, 1962   126,930
13. Rangers v Celtic, 1966   126,552
14. Rangers v Celtic, 1973   122,714
15. Rangers v Dundee, 1964   120,982
16. Rangers v Celtic, 1963 (replay)   120,263
17. Celtic v Rangers, 1971   120,092
18. Rangers v East Fife, 1950   118,262
19. Rangers v Celtic, 1928   118,115
20. Kilmarnock v Rangers, 1929   114,708

The atmosphere at a Cup final at Hampden Park is something special even though for safety reasons the capacity has been considerably reduced from the 150,000 maximum established in 1937. The stadium we know today is actually the third Hampden. Queen's Park vacated the first in 1883 when a new railway was being built, and the second in 1903 to move to larger premises. The second Hampden changed its name to New Cathkin Park and became the home of Third Lanark. It remains one of the strangest sights in football to see Queen's Park playing a Second Division match in front of a few hundred spectators dotted around the vast open spaces of Hampden Park. If you want to talk to the chap next to you, you need a loud-hailer!

THE 12 MOST SUCCESSFUL SCOTTISH FA CUP CLUBS OVER THE PAST DECADE

		Number of ties won
1.	Celtic	35
2.	Aberdeen	27
	Dundee United	27
4.	Heart of Midlothian	22
5.	Rangers	20
6.	Motherwell	18
7.	St Mirren	17
8.	Dundee	16
9.	Alloa Athletic	15
	East Fife	15
	St Johnstone	15
12.	Hibernian	13

As you can see, Rangers have had a pretty lean time of it lately in the Scottish Cup. Last season's triumph was their first since 1981. Hearts are the nearly team of Scottish football. In 1986, they came agonisingly close to doing the double but ended up with nothing. They went into the last day of the League season two points ahead of Celtic and with a four-goal advantage in goal difference. Yet while Celtic were romping home 5-0 at St Mirren, Hearts contrived to concede two late goals at Dundee and lost 2-0. Suddenly Celtic had a three-goal better goal difference and the title was theirs. Just to rub salt into the wound, the distraught Hearts players crumbled 3-0 to Aberdeen in the Cup final a week later. To long-suffering Hearts fans, it brought back unwanted memories of 1965 when they again blew the League title in spectacular fashion on the last day of the season. The race was between them and Kilmarnock and the pair met at Tynecastle. Hearts were two points clear and so needed only a draw to take the championship. They lost 2-0 and missed the title by one goal. If they had lost 2-1 or 1-0, they would still have been champions. It was that close. All in all, it's a wonder any Hearts fans survived to see the action replay 21 years on. Mind you, there was an occasion when maybe Hearts did feel a bit too sorry for themselves. After being beaten by Vale of Leven in an early Cup tie, they protested about the result 'on account of the utter incapability of the referee owing to a physical infirmity of defective eyesight.' The ref duly produced a medical certificate from an eye specialist and Hearts were made to apologise!

THE 12 LEAST SUCCESSFUL SCOTTISH FA CUP CLUBS OVER THE PAST DECADE

		Number of ties won
1.	Kilmarnock	2
2.	Montrose	3
3.	Clyde	5
	Falkirk	5
	Hamilton Academicals	5
	Partick Thistle	5
	Raith Rovers	5
	Stenhousemuir	5
9.	Arbroath	6
	Ayr United	6
	Dumbarton	6
12.	Meadowbank Thistle	7
	Queen's Park	7

CHAPTER FOUR
FROM ANFIED TO GAYFIELD

THE FIRST ENGLISH AND SCOTTISH LEAGUE CLUBS TO INSTAL FLOODLIGHTS

1.	Oxford United (then known as Headington)	December 1950
2.	Swindon Town	April 1951
3.	Arsenal	September 1951
4.	Southampton	October 1951
5.	Stenhousemuir	November 1951
6.	Carlisle United	February 1952
7.	Sunderland	December 1952
8.	Bristol City	January 1953
	Hull City	January 1953
9.	Doncaster Rovers	February 1953
	Newcastle United	February 1953
11.	Derby County	March 1953
	Grimsby Town	March 1953
	Hereford United	March 1953
	Notts County	March 1953
15.	West Ham United	April 1953

The very first floodlit match actually took place back in October 1878 when two Sheffield representative teams met at Bramall Lane before a crowd of 20,000. The four lights were mounted on 30-foot poles and produced power to the equivalent of 8,000 candles. The experiment was so successful that others followed suit. In Scotland, Third Lanark entertained Vale of Leven in a floodlit friendly where a single beam, mounted on a platform, was directed at the ball to spotlight the play. But at Chorley, Lancashire, a crowd of 8,000 went home disappointed after waiting two hours in torrential rain. The electrician couldn't switch on the lights! The first current League club to instal lights were Oxford United (then known as Headington United). They played Banbury Spencer in a charity match in December 1950, having borrowed the lamps from buildings all over Oxford. Finally the FA lifted its long-standing ban on competitive floodlit matches and Southampton Reserves met Spurs Reserves in a Football Combination fixture at The Dell on 1 October 1951. Afterwards the Southampton manager, Sid Cann, prophesied: 'Floodlit soccer has come to stay.' Sid Cann was right although not all of the big clubs caught on immediately. Manchester United didn't instal lights until 1957 and so had to play their early European Cup ties at Maine Road.

THE LAST ENGLISH AND SCOTTISH LEAGUE CLUBS TO INSTAL FLOODLIGHTS

1.	Stranraer	1981
2.	Alloa Athletic	1979
3.	Brechin City	1977
4.	Berwick Rangers	1972
5	Forfar Athletic	October 1971
	Montrose	October 1971
7.	Hamilton Academicals	March 1971
8.	Ayr United	1970
9.	Albion Rovers	1968
	Cowdenbeath	1968
11.	Chesterfield	1967
12.	Clydebank	1965
	Hartlepool United	1965
14.	St Johnstone	1964
15.	Gillingham	1963
16.	Dundee United	1962
	Fulham	1962
	Lincoln City	1962

Bournemouth's first floodlit venture was an eventful affair. It was a League game against Northampton in 1961 but the lights failed just before kick-off and the match was delayed for an hour. Other clubs who didn't instal lights until 1961 were Halifax, Huddersfield, Brighton, Charlton, Stirling Albion, Oldham, Mansfield and Nottingham Forest. Apart from Fulham, Forest were the last First Division club to have lights. Perhaps the saddest switch-on story comes from Arbroath. Their proud new lights were displayed against Dundee United in 1955, but one of the lamps was smashed by a mighty clearance from an Arbroath player. I wonder if the club sent him the bill.

THE 12 LARGEST FOOTBALL LEAGUE PITCHES

		Sq. yards
1.	Carlisle United	9126
2.	Scarborough	9000
3.	Nottingham Forest	8970
4.	Manchester City	8968
5.	Cardiff City	8892
	Leeds United	8892
7.	Manchester United	8816
	Port Vale	8816
	Shrewsbury Town	8816
10.	Chester City (at Macclesfield)	8800
	Leyton Orient	8800
12.	Blackburn Rovers	8740

West Brom's pitch used to be a massive 127 x 87 yards (that's 11049 square yards) – I for one wouldn't have fancied running up and down that for 90 minutes. Greavsie would never have made it out of the centre circle! More recently, Doncaster Rovers boasted the biggest pitch until manager Billy Bremner decided, in an effort to improve the club's fortunes, to lop eight yards off the length. Judging by their results last season, they'd better try taking off another eight.

THE 12 SMALLEST FOOTBALL
LEAGUE PITCHES

		Sq. yards
1.	Halifax Town	7700
2.	Arsenal	7810
	Colchester United	7810
4.	Ipswich Town	7840
5.	Wrexham	7881
6.	Luton Town	7920
	Preston North End	7920
	Sheffield United	7920
	Southampton	7920
10.	Tranmere Rovers	7952
11.	Tottenham Hotspur	8030
12.	Bury	8064
	Chesterfield	8064
	Queen's Park Rangers	8064
	West Ham United	8064

When Arsenal played their first game at Highbury, against Leicester Fosse in 1913, the ground was still in the throes of completion. It was said to be like playing in a builder's yard. The facilities certainly weren't up to much – a player who was injured in that game had to be carried away on a milk cart!

THE 10 LARGEST SCOTTISH LEAGUE PITCHES

		Sq. yards
1.	Dundee	8855
2.	Stenhousemuir	8814
3.	Celtic	8625
	Queen's Park	8625
	Rangers	8625
	St Johnstone	8625
7.	Berwick Rangers	8512
8.	Kilmarnock	8395
9.	Hibernian	8288
10.	Alloa Athletic	8250
	Dumbarton	8250
	Motherwell	8250

THE 10 SMALLEST SCOTTISH LEAGUE PITCHES

		Sq. yards
1.	Brechin City	7370
2.	Clydebank	7480
3.	Airdrieonians	7504
4.	Meadowbank Thistle	7560
5.	Raith Rovers	7571
6.	Partick Thistle	7632
7.	Albion Rovers	7700
	Cowdenbeath	7700
	Falkirk	7700
	Hamilton Academicals (shared by Clyde)	7700
	Stranraer	7700

WHERE THEY ONCE PLAYED

Olive Grove (Sheffield Wednesday)
Cockle's Field (Bolton Wanderers)
The Nest (Norwich City)
Blinkbonny (Falkirk)
The Trotting Track (Stranraer)
The Prairie (Mansfield Town)
Park Royal (Queen's Park Rangers)
Steele's Field (Tranmere Rovers)
Raikes Hall Gardens (Blackpool)
Old Mavisbank (Airdrieonians)
The Antelope Ground (Southampton)
The Chuckery (Walsall)
Sands Brae (Raith Rovers)
The Old Archery Ground (Middlesbrough)
The Chanonry (Aberdeen)
Parker's Piece (Cambridge United)
Muntz St (Birmingham City)
The Memorial Ground (West Ham United)
Acton Park (Wrexham)
Shortroods (St Mirren)
Bull Stob Close (Berwick Rangers)
Anfield (Everton)

Yes, as every Merseysider knows, Everton were the original tenants of Anfield. They played there between 1884 and 1892 until falling out with their landlord, local MP John Houlding, over a rent increase. Houlding gave them notice to quit and established his own club, Liverpool FC, at Anfield. He had wanted to keep the name Everton but the Football League refused to let him do so. Meanwhile the organist at St Domingo's church (Everton had been called St Domingo's) told the Everton committee that he had an option on a field on the other side of Stanley Park. So Everton moved there and that barren field was transformed into Goodison Park. Who knows, if Houlding hadn't been so mean about the rent, Liverpool FC might never have existed. And if there had been a second club in the city, it would probably have been Bootle.

FOOTBALL LEAGUE CLUBS WITH UNDERSOIL HEATING

Arsenal
Blackburn Rovers
Bolton Wanderers
Derby County
Everton
Leeds United
Liverpool
Manchester City
Manchester United
Newcastle United
Sheffield Wednesday
Tottenham Hotspur

Getting a pitch playable has always been a problem. Straw was always a favourite for combatting frost while in the old days, cattle would be brought in to graze on the pitch in mid-week, to save cutting the grass. Fine in practice but pity the poor goalkeeper going up for a high ball and not being sure what he would be landing in. Arsenal were one of the pioneers of undersoil heating – they installed an electric wiring system in 1964 at a cost of £15,000. It was money well spent. In Scotland, Hibernian were the first club to fit undersoil heating, in June 1980. In fact, Hibs are real trailblazers. They were the first Scottish club to wear a sponsor's name on their shirts and, in 1983, they became the first Scottish club to instal an electric scoreboard.

THE 15 NEWEST LEAGUE GROUNDS

1. Walsall (Bescot Stadium)   1990
2. St Johnstone (McDiarmid Park)   1989
3. Scunthorpe United (Glanford Park)   1988
4. Meadowbank Thistle (Meadowbank Stadium)   1970
5. Southend United (Roots Hall)   1955
6. Berwick Rangers (New Shielfield Park)   1954
7. Port Vale (Vale Park)   1950
8. Hull City (Boothferry Park)   1946
   Stirling Albion (Annfield Park)   1946
10. Clydebank (New Kilbowie Park)   1937
11. Norwich City (Carrow Road)   1935
12. Cambridge United (Abbey Stadium)   1932
    York City (Bootham Crescent)   1932
14. Crystal Palace (Selhurst Park)   1924
15. Manchester City (Maine Road)   1923

Norwich City's old ground, The Nest, was notorious for subsidence, so much so that the groundsman had to warn players to be on their guard when taking corners. If they weren't careful, they could disappear down a vast hole, possibly never to re-surface. Finally, in May 1935, the FA informed the club that the ground was no longer suitable. This left Norwich with just three months to find and build a new ground before the start of the next season. They were offered a site on Carrow Road and incredibly got it ready in time to accommodate a crowd of nearly 30,000 for their opening game against West Ham on 31 August.

THE 10 LEAGUE CLUBS WHO HAVE BEEN LONGEST AT THE SAME GROUND

1. Stoke City (The Victoria Ground)   since 1878
2. Dumbarton (Boghead Park)   1879
3. Preston North End (Deepdale)   1881
4. Burnley (Turf Moor)   1882
   Falkirk (Brockville Park)   1882
6. Darlington (Feethams)   1883
   Morton (Cappielow Park)   1883
8. Chesterfield (Saltergate)   1884
9. Bury (Gigg Lane)   1885
   Dunfermline Athletic (East End Park)   1885

Falkirk actually first played at Brockville back in 1876 but three years later they moved out for a few seasons before returning in 1882. Similarly Morton made their bow at Cappielow in 1879 but interrupted their unbroken tenure by straying to Ladyburn for the 1882-83 season. Dumbarton's ground at Boghead used to have what must have been the smallest main stand at any recognised League ground. Just 25 feet long, it was known affectionately as the Postage Box. It would barely have accommodated one of Malcolm Allison's cigars! Sadly, the Postage Box was demolished in 1979 to make way for a new stand.

MOST ISOLATED BRITISH LEAGUE GROUNDS

1. Carlisle United   (58 miles from Newcastle United)
2. Berwick Rangers   (48 miles from Hibernian/Meadowbank)
3. Hereford United   (43 miles from Bristol City)
    Stranraer   (43 miles from Ayr United)
5. Norwich City   (42 miles from Ipswich Town)
6. Brighton & Hove Albion   (39 miles from Crystal Palace)
7. Scarborough   (36 miles from York City)
8. Swansea City   (34 miles from Cardiff City)
9. Aberdeen   (33 miles from Montrose)
10. Peterborough United (32 miles from Cambridge United)

There's no place like home – unless you're Maidstone United, that is. They played their home games at Dartford which is 25 miles away from Maidstone. And once a year, they were closer to home when they were away! That's when they travelled to Gillingham for their local 'derby'. For Gillingham is considerably nearer to Maidstone than Dartford is. As for that lovely rural outpost of Carlisle (the only ground where you used to get stick from the sheep in the field behind the goal if you missed a sitter), that is nearer to a Scottish club, Queen of the South in Dumfries, than to any in England. One of the great things about long away trips is the card school. Shanks used to enjoy a game of cards – until he was skinned at blind three-card brag by Bobby Graham on a trip to Newcastle. Shanks was livid at losing and when Bobby bravely went to collect his winnings from him on Monday, Shanks told him in no uncertain terms: 'No more cards. That gambling is bad for you. Cut it out!'

NEAREST BRITISH LEAGUE GROUNDS

1.	Dundee and Dundee United	200 yards
2.	Nottingham Forest and Notts County	330 yards
3.	Falkirk and East Stirlingshire	800 yards
4.	Liverpool and Everton	840 yards
5.	Hibernian and Meadowbank Thistle	880 yards

SAME GROUND – DIFFERENT NAME

Old name	Present name
The Celery Trenches	Abbey Stadium (Cambridge United)
Walnut St	Filbert St (Leicester City)
Old Town Ditch Field	Vetch Field (Swansea City)
Mere Green	Goodison Park (Everton)
Clepington Park	Tannadice Park (Dundee United)
St Clements	Spotland (Rochdale)
Owlerton	Hillsborough (Sheffield Wednesday)
Low Pasture	Belle Vue (Doncaster Rovers)
Boulton Paul Sports Ground	Carrow Road (Norwich City)

Somehow a trip to Old Town Ditch Field or The Celery Trenches doesn't sound too enticing. They sound more like venues for Gardeners' World than Match of the Day. Swansea's Old Town Ditch Field was used for growing vetch, hence the change of name to something a little easier on the tongue. The Celery Trenches got its name because it was the site of a collection of allotments. Indeed, one end of the Abbey Stadium is known today as the Allotment End.

FIRST LEAGUE GROUNDS WITH ARTIFICIAL PITCHES

1. Queen's Park Rangers   1981
2. Luton Town   1985
3. Preston North End   1986
4. Oldham Athletic   1986
5. Stirling Albion   1987

Queen's Park Rangers' experiment with an artificial pitch marked the latest chapter in the bewildering story of their home venues. For over the years, they have had no fewer than 14 homes, more than any other Football League club. They started out in 1885, formed by pupils at Droop Street School, part of St Jude's Institute on the Queen's Park Estate in West London. They were known as St Jude's Institute and played at Kensal Rise. Soon they moved to Brondesbury and then Welford's Fields and in 1898 finally adopted their present name. But they continued to wander, seemingly playing on every expanse of grass in the area. Subsequently the cuckoos of football have lodged at such places as Stamford Bridge, Highbury, Park Royal and, for two separate periods, the White City. It's a wonder their players ever turned up for a game.

LEAGUE CLUBS WHOSE GROUNDS WERE BOMBED DURING THE SECOND WORLD WAR

Arsenal
Birmingham City
Bristol City
Charlton Athletic
Coventry City
Derby County
Everton
Fulham
Manchester United
Millwall
Nottingham Forest
Notts County
Plymouth Argyle
Sheffield United
Sheffield Wednesday
Southampton
Sunderland
Tranmere Rovers
West Ham United
York City

Unluckiest of all were Hartlepool United, the only club to be bombed during the First World War – and that was a complete accident. A pair of German Zeppelins were intercepted while trying to raid the town. They were shot down into the North Sea but as they did so, they released their deadly load of 100 bombs, two of which, by pure chance, landed fair and square on the stand at the Victoria Ground. After the war, United demanded compensation from the German government but not only did their pleas fall on deaf ears, they also clearly upset the Hun because during the Second World War, the town was attacked again and German bombs only just missed the Victoria Ground

10 FORMER SITES

The following grounds were built on unusual sites:

The Dell (Southampton) – a duckpond
Springfield Park (Wigan Athletic) – horse-trotting track
Maine Road (Manchester City) – claypit
Villa Park (Aston Villa) – amusement park
Fratton Park (Portsmouth) – market garden
St James's Park (Exeter City) – pig-grazing land
Gay Meadow (Shrewsbury Town) – open-air theatre
Upton Park (West Ham United) – cabbage patch
White Hart Lane (Tottenham Hotspur) – nursery
Pittodrie (Aberdeen) – dung heap

It's true. Aberdeen play on what was once a dung heap used by the local police, Pittodrie being Celtic for 'place of manure'. No doubt after a heavy home defeat, the locals would agree.

5 GROUNDS BUILT ON RUBBISH TIPS

Burnden Park (Bolton Wanderers)
Ninian Park (Cardiff City)
Roots Hall (Southend United)
The Shay (Halifax Town)
The Victoria Ground (Hartlepool United)

When Cardiff turned professional in 1910 and moved to Ninian Park, the players found that their new status didn't exactly bring in untold glamour. There were no boutiques or discos to open for them – not even a decent supermarket. Instead one of their first chores was to clear the pitch of broken glass and litter, the remains of the rubbish tip. They probably employed the sweeper system.

BRITISH LEAGUE GROUNDS WHICH ARE FURTHEST FROM A RAILWAY STATION

1. Forfar Athletic   14 miles from Dundee and Arbroath
2. Brechin City   8 miles from Montrose
   East Fife   8 miles from Kirkcaldy
4. Mansfield Town   7½ miles from Alfreton and Mansfield
5. Alloa Athletic   7 miles from Stirling

Being near to a railway station can be beneficial to clubs. The story goes that a former manager of Halifax used to get incoming players to sign for the club at the station before they had a chance to see the ground! Some clubs have their own station adjoining the ground – Arsenal, Derby, Exeter and Hull for example. Herbert Chapman even had the old underground station Gillespie Road renamed Arsenal. Another early venture was West Bromwich Albion's Hawthorns Halt, opened in 1934. But that closed in 1968. Of the clubs without their own special halt, probably the nearest to a main-line station are Hamilton and Falkirk, both about 100 yards away, closely followed by Brighton, Crewe, Charlton and Shrewsbury. That's good news for, as any football fan will tell you, it can be a mighty long trek to grounds located in the far-flung corners of town like Doncaster's Belle Vue, Bristol City's Ashton Gate, Colchester's Layer Road or Sheffield Wednesday's Hillsborough. And it's even worse walking back if you've lost…

TOP 20 CLUB RECORD ATTENDANCES – FOOTBALL LEAGUE

1. Manchester City	84,569
2. Chelsea	82,905
3. Everton	78,299
4. Aston Villa	76,588
5. Sunderland	75,118
6. Tottenham Hotspur	75,038
7. Charlton Athletic	75,031
8. Arsenal	73,295
9. Sheffield Wednesday	72,841
10. Manchester United	70,504
11. Bolton Wanderers	69,912
12. Newcastle United	68,386
13. Sheffield United	68,287
14. Huddersfield Town	67,037
15. Birmingham City	66,844
16. West Bromwich Albion	64,815
17. Liverpool	61,905
18. Blackburn Rovers	61,783
19. Wolverhampton Wanderers	61,315
20. Cardiff City	57,893

Ground capacities are constantly changing. Manchester United's is being drastically reduced for 1992-93 but when the work is finished, Old Trafford will, at around 45,000, still rank as one of the largest, along with Highbury and Maine Road. It could be argued that the 1967 Merseyside 'derby' attracted the largest crowd of all because it was watched by 105,000 people. 64,381 watched the actual game at Goodison Park while another 40,169 gathered to see it on closed circuit TV at Anfield. Imagine that many people crowded around a huge television screen. Greavsie reckons half of them were waiting for Coronation Street!

BOTTOM 20 CLUB RECORD ATTENDANCES – FOOTBALL LEAGUE

1.	Barnet	11,026
2.	Scarborough	11,130
3.	Cambridge United	14,000
4.	Hartlepool United	17,426
5.	Wimbledon	18,000
6.	Hereford United	18,114
7.	Shrewsbury Town	18,917
8.	Colchester United	19,073
9.	Crewe Alexandra	20,000
10.	Chester City	20,500
11.	Exeter City	20,984
12.	Darlington	21,023
13.	Torquay United	21,908
14.	Oxford United	22,750
15.	Gillingham	23,002
16.	Lincoln City	23,196
17.	Scunthorpe United	23,935
18.	Rochdale	24,231
19.	Tranmere Rovers	24,424
20.	Mansfield Town	24,467

Again, current capacities are much lower. For example, Maidstone's home at Watling Street, Dartford, only held 5,252 and several other grounds (Blackpool, Bury, Cambridge United, Crewe, Darlington, Halifax, Scarborough, Scunthorpe, Stockport, Torquay and Bristol Rovers' residence at Twerton Park, Bath) all have capacities of under 10,000. The lowest official attendance for a Football League game was the 450 who poured through the turnstiles to watch Rochdale entertain Cambridge United in the Third Division in 1974. It's often claimed that only 13 people saw Stockport play Leicester at Old Trafford in 1921 but those present insist that as many as 2,000 were inside. Obviously the gate-man nodded off.

TOP 12 RECORD CLUB
ATTENDANCES – SCOTLAND

1.	Rangers	118,567
2.	Queen's Park	95,722
3.	Celtic	92,000
4.	Hibernian	65,860
5.	Heart of Midlothian	53,496
6.	Clyde	52,000
7.	Partick Thistle	49,838
8.	St Mirren	47,438
9.	Aberdeen	45,061
10.	Dundee	43,024
11.	Motherwell	35,632
12.	Kilmarnock	34,246

BOTTOM 12 RECORD CLUB
ATTENDANCES – SCOTLAND

1.	Meadowbank Thistle	4,000
2.	Stranraer	6,500
3.	Brechin City	8,122
4.	Montrose	8,983
5.	Forfar Athletic	10,800
6.	East Stirlingshire	11,500
7.	Stenhousemuir	12,500
8.	Alloa Athletic	13,000
9.	Berwick Rangers	13,365
10.	Arbroath	13,510
11.	Clydebank	14,900
12.	Dumbarton	18,001

O nly 32 people bothered to go and watch East Stirlingshire play Leith in a Second Division match in 1939 – the lowest gate for any League game in Britain. Bryan Robson gets more than that turn up to see him mow his lawn.

ODD ENDS

The following are all parts of League grounds:

The British Coal Opencast Stand (Port Vale)
The Findus Stand (Grimsby Town)
The Ducket (Berwick Rangers)
The T.C. Keay End (Dundee)
The Rookery (Watford)
The Wee Dublin End (Morton)
The Cowshed (Exeter City)
The Jungle (Celtic)
Bob Bank (Cardiff City)
The Sainsbury's End (Crystal Palace)
The Cemetery End (Brechin City)

C ardiff's Bob Bank is so called because it used to cost a shilling to stand there while Morton's Wee Dublin End gets its name from the Irish families who once lived in prefabricated bungalows behind that end of the ground. And what could be more inspiring than Brechin's Cemetery End? You're two down at half-time, it's pouring with rain, the wind is howling, but it doesn't matter because you're attacking The Cemetery End in the second half. The opposition's got no chance...

LEAGUE GROUNDS THAT ARE NEAREST TO THE SEA

1.	Arbroath	50 yards
2.	Grimsby Town	150 yards
3.	Aberdeen	300 yards
4.	Hartlepool United	350 yards
5.	Swansea City	400 yards
6.	Blackpool	420 yards
7.	East Fife	440 yards
8.	Sunderland	520 yards

Arbroath's proximity to the North Sea is something of a mixed blessing. It means that Gayfield remains relatively frost-free and is therefore often playable when most other grounds in Scotland aren't, but at the same time the way the wind whips off the North Sea means that spectators often need thermal underwear and a hip-flask even in August.

10 GROUNDS SITUATED NEAR RIVERS

Blackburn Rovers (Darwen)
Carlisle United (Petteril)
Darlington (Skerne)
Norwich City (Wensum)
Nottingham Forest (Trent)
Peterborough United (Nene)
Sheffield Wednesday (Don)
Shrewsbury Town (Severn)
Stenhousemuir (Jenny's Burn)
Stoke City (Trent)

Apart from the Thames flowing past Craven Cottage, football's most famous river has always been the Severn onto which

113

Shrewsbury's Gay Meadow backs. It requires nothing more than a hefty clearance for the ball to land in the Severn. Footballs are expensive and for years the club paid Fred Davies to sit in a coracle and retrieve them at 25 p a time. But Fred wasn't infallible – the story goes that he once fished a swan out of the river by mistake. Two legs, feathers and a beak – hard to confuse it with a football. Still if his eyesight was that dodgy, it's as well there weren't many bald men swimming in the Severn.

---

10 GROUNDS FROM WHERE YOU CAN SEE A CHURCH OR CATHEDRAL

Aston Villa
Brechin City
Everton
Heart of Midlothian
Hereford United
Lincoln City
Rochdale
Sheffield United
Stockport County
York City

The best-known church in football is that of St Luke the Evangelist which nestles in a corner of Goodison Park. Everton once tried to have it moved so that they could develop that part of the ground but their prayers were answered in the negative. I for one think it would be a great shame if it were ever to go.

20 MORE FORMER GROUNDS

The Cow Pat (Lincoln City)
Broom Hill (Ipswich Town)
The Kursaal Ground (Southend United)
Siemens Meadow (Charlton Athletic)
The Tryst (Stenhousemuir)
Bent Farm (Hamilton Academicals)
The Croft (Swindon Town)
Old Sheds Field (Crewe Alexandra)
Cowheath Park (Albion Rovers)
Four Acres (West Bromwich Albion)
Horatio St (Sunderland)
Holm Quarry (Kilmarnock)
The Invicta Ground (Arsenal)
Dowells Field (Coventry City)
Spital (Chesterfield)
West Craigie (Dundee)
Whipcord Lane (Chester City)
Benns Field (Brentford)
Kinning Park (Rangers)
Whittles Whippet Ground (Leyton Orient)

I've just discovered my biggest regret in football – that I never got to play at Whittles Whippet Ground. Mind you, Orient were there at the end of the 19th century...and I wasn't around then. I think even Greavsie was only playing youth football at the time.

CHAPTER FIVE

PLAYER POWER

MOST SENIOR LEAGUE APPEARANCES

(Up to end of 1991-92)

1. Peter Shilton   968   (Leicester City, Stoke City, Nottingham Forest, Southampton, Derby County, Plymouth Argyle: 1966 -)

2. Tommy Hutchison   854   (Alloa Athletic, Blackpool, Coventry City, Manchester City, Burnley, Swansea City: 1968-90)

3. Terry Paine   824   (Southampton, Hereford United: 1957-77)

4. Alan Oakes   777   (Manchester City, Chester, Port Vale: 1959-84)

5. John Trollope   770   (all with Swindon Town: 1960-80)

6. Jimmy Dickinson   764   (all with Portsmouth: 1946-65)

7. Roy Sproson   761   (all with Port Vale: 1950-72)

8. Billy Bonds   758   (Charlton Athletic, West Ham United: 1965-88)

    Ray Clemence   758   (Scunthorpe United, Liverpool, Tottenham Hotspur: 1966-87)

10. Pat Jennings   757   (Watford, Tottenham Hotspur, Arsenal: 1963-84)

    Frank Worthington   757   (Huddersfield Town, Leicester City, Bolton Wanderers, Birmingham City, Leeds United, Sunderland, Southampton, Brighton & Hove Albion, Tranmere Rovers, Preston North End, Stockport County: 1967-88)

G reavsie reckons Pat Jennings was one of the quickest players on the Spurs staff. In practice matches, Pat used to play up front while Greavsie went in goal. That's something I would like to have seen! Before turning professional with Watford, Pat had a job as a milkman. But the man who went on to earn a worldwide reputation as a keeper with big, safe hands wasn't as steady when it came to handling gold tops. Once as he jumped off the milk cart to deliver a couple of pints, he caught his trouser buttons on the top of a crate. The result was three crates of broken milk bottles all over the road. His boss was not pleased.

MOST LEAGUE GOALS IN A CAREER

1. Arthur Rowley   434   (West Bromwich Albion, Fulham, Leicester City, Shrewsbury Town: 1946-65)
2. Jimmy McGrory   410   (Celtic, Clydebank: 1922-38)
3. Hughie Gallacher   387   (Airdieonians, Newcastle United, Chelsea, Derby County, Notts County, Grimsby Town, Gateshead: 1921-39)
4. Dixie Dean   379   (Tranmere Rovers, Everton, Notts County: 1923-37)
5. Hugh Ferguson   362   (Motherwell, Cardiff City, Dundee: 1916-30)
6. Jimmy Greaves   357   (Chelsea, Tottenham Hotspur, West Ham United: 1957-71)
7. Steve Bloomer   352   (Derby County (2 spells), Middlesbrough; 1892-1914)
8. George Camsell   348   (Durham City, Middlesbrough: 1923-39)
9. Dave Halliday   338   (St Mirren, Dundee, Sunderland, Arsenal, Manchester City, Clapton Orient: 1920-35)
10. John Atyeo   315   (all with Bristol City: 1951-66)
     Joe Smith   315   (Bolton Wanderers, Stockport County: 1908-29)

Some great players here – even the bloke at number six. I shan't talk about him because it will go to his head but he was a fine illustration of the fact that goalscorers don't have to be big. Another example was Hughie Gallacher, one of Scotland's wonderful Wembley Wizards. He remembered when he came south to make his debut for Newcastle in 1926, as he ran out onto the pitch, the crowd let out a mass gasp of disappointment. They thought he was far too small. They soon changed their minds. Joe Smith went on to be a successful manager with Blackpool for 23 years, from 1935 to 1958. Luckily, his command of soccer tactics was superior to his command of the English language. He was renowned for his malapropisms. One classic was when he attempted to describe the tremendous club spirit at Bloomfield Road. He insisted: 'We've got perfect harmonium in the dressing room.'

---

8 GOALSCORING GOALKEEPERS

The following goalkeepers have all scored with long clearances:

Pat Jennings (Tottenham Hotspur) v Manchester United, 1967
Peter Shilton (Leicester City) v Southampton, 1967
Ray Cashley (Bristol City) v Hull City, 1973
Steve Sherwood (Watford) v Coventry City, 1984
Steve Ogrizovic (Coventry City) v Sheffield Wednesday, 1986
Andy Goram (Hibernian) v Morton, 1988
Alan Peterson (Glentoran) v Linfield, 1989
Ray Charles (East Fife) v Stranraer, 1990

I can see Greavsie's face now – only the Scots could have a goalkeeper called Ray Charles! Well in actual fact, although he plays in Scotland, Ray is English. He was born in Leicester. Being beaten from the other end of the field is the sort of thing that can happen to any keeper…but usually only once. However Linfield's

Irish international custodian George Dunlop can vow that lightning is perfectly capable of striking twice. When Glentoran's Alan Peterson baffled him in the Roadferry Cup Final, it was the second time in just over a year that poor George had lost out to his opposing number one. For in 1988, Cliftonville's Andy Mc Lean did exactly the same – and what's more it was Andy's Irish League debut.

FASTEST GOALS CLAIMED

(A couple of these may have to be taken with a large pinch of salt)

		Seconds
1.	Colin Cowperthwaite (Barrow) v Kettering Town, 1979	3 ½
2.	Jim Fryatt (Bradford P.A. v Tranmere Rovers, 1965	4
3.	Malcolm Macdonald (Newcastle Utd) v St Johnstone, 1972	5
4.	Barrie Jones (Newport County) v Torquay United, 1962	6
	Tommy Langley (Q.P.R.) v Bolton Wanderers, 1980	6
	Albert Mundy (Aldershot) v Hartlepools United, 1958	6
	Keith Smith (Crystal Palace) v Derby County, 1964	6
8.	William Sharp (Partick Thistle) v Queen of the South, 1947	7

The top two are certainly open to dispute, particularly since Jim Fryatt's goal was scored after three other players had already touched the ball! Malcolm Macdonald's effort in a pre-season friendly remains the fastest to be timed officially. When West Ham entertained West Brom in a First Division game in 1931, Albion's Billy Richardson scored four in the first five minutes. Albion slowed down after that, adding just one more for a 5-1 victory. Me? I was usually too busy looking for friends and family in the stand for the first five minutes.

THE FIRST MILLION POUND BRITISH PLAYERS

1. Trevor Francis (Birmingham to Nottingham Forest, Feb 1979)
2. Steve Daley (Wolves to Manchester City, Sept 1979)
3. Andy Gray (Aston Villa to Wolves, Sept 1979)
4. Kevin Reeves (Norwich City to Manchester City, March 1980)
5. Clive Allen (Q.P.R. to Arsenal, June 1980)
6. Ian Wallace (Coventry to Nottingham Forest, July 1980)
7. Clive Allen (Arsenal to Crystal Palace, Aug 1980)
   Kenny Sansom (Crystal Palace to Arsenal, Aug 1980)
9. Garry Birtles (Nottingham Forest to Manchester Utd, Oct 1980)
10. Justin Fashanu (Norwich City to Nottingham Forest, Aug 1981)

Brian Clough featured heavily in the early million pound deals and he's the first to admit that of the three players he signed, only Trevor Francis really justified the fee. Mind you, Cloughie did pretty well with Garry Birtles, selling him on to Manchester United for £1,250,000. And all that after an inauspicious first trip to see Birtles playing for non-league Long Eaton United. Cloughie later remarked that the half-time cup of Bovril had been better than Birtles that day.

EARLY BRITISH TRANSFER MILESTONES

£100	Willie Groves (West Bromwich Albion to Aston Villa, 1892)
£500	Alf Common (Sheffield United to Sunderland, 1902)
£1,000	Alf Common (Sunderland to Middlesbrough, 1905)
£2,000	Danny Shea (West Ham United to Blackburn Rovers, 1912)
£5,000	Syd Puddefoot (West Ham United to Falkirk, 1922)
£10,000	David Jack (Bolton Wanderers to Arsenal, 1928)
£20,000	Tommy Lawton (Chelsea to Notts County, 1947)
£50,000	Denis Law (Huddersfield Town to Manchester City, 1960)
£100,000	Denis Law (Torino to Manchester United, 1962)
£200,000	Martin Peters (West Ham Utd to Tottenham Hotspur, 1970)
£500,000	David Mills (Middlesbrough to West Bromwich Albion, 1979)

I had the privilege of playing alongside Denis Law for Scotland. What a great player and what a patriot – he tells me the blackest day of his life was in 1966 when he heard that England had won the World Cup! So Denis was thrilled to be a member of the Scotland team which hammered England 3-2 at Wembley, a year later in 1967. We claim we beat the World Cup winners but Greavsie has a theory that renowned Scots-hater Alf Ramsey might have seen it coming. That's why Ramsey picked Greavsie instead of Geoff Hurst against the Scots so that in case England lost, Ramsey could turn round and say that it wasn't the World Cup winning team. Knowing Alf Ramsey, I'd believe it too.

SENT OFF AT WEMBLEY

Boris Stankovic (Yugoslavia) v Sweden,
    Olympic Games 1948
Antonio Rattin (Argentina) v England, World Cup 1966
Billy Bremner (Leeds United) v Liverpool,
    FA Charity Shield 1974
Kevin Keegan (Liverpool) v Leeds United,
    FA Charity Shield 1974
Gilbert Dresch (Luxembourg) v England, 1977
Kevin Moran (Manchester United) v Everton,
    FA Cup Final 1985

A guy who made Rattin look like a choirboy was Frank Barson who played for a whole host of clubs between the wars. He was sent off and suspended so many times, the authorities lost count. Playing for Watford, he was once banned for seven months and he is even said to have pulled a gun on his manager at Aston Villa! Barson would have felt at home in a local cup match between Tongham Youth Club of Surrey and Hampshire side Hawley in 1969. The referee ended up booking all 22 players, including one who was carted off to hospital, and one of the linesmen. In a splendid understatement, one of the players said afterwards: 'It was a good, hard game.'

MOST FOOTBALL LEAGUE GOALS IN A SEASON

1. Dixie Dean (Everton, 1927-28)   60
2. George Camsell (Middlesbrough, 1926-27)   59
3. Ted Harston (Mansfield Town, 1936-37)   55
   Joe Payne (Luton Town, 1936-37)   55
5. Terry Bly (Peterborough United, 1960-61)   52
6. Clarrie Bourton (Coventry City, 1931-32)   49
   Pongo Waring (Aston Villa, 1930-31)   49
8. Harry Morris (Swindon Town, 1926-27)   47
9. Derek Dooley (Sheffield Wednesday, 1951-52)   46
   Alf Lythgoe (Stockport County, 1933-34)   46
   Peter Simpson (Crystal Palace, 1930-31)   46

George Camsell's scoring record looked set to last for years but was broken within 12 months by the legendary Dixie Dean. Going into their final game at home to Arsenal, Everton were already sure of the First Division championship but Dixie needed a hat-trick to overhaul Camsell's total. Arsenal went a goal up inside two minutes but 60 seconds later, Dixie equalised. Three minutes later he converted a penalty to equal Camsell's record. For the rest of the match, his team-mates tried everything to lay on a goal for him but as the minutes ticked by, it looked as though it would all be in vain. But then with eight minutes remaining, Dixie headed home a cross and the record was his. Dixie was a hero on Merseyside and died in the most fitting way imaginable, watching the 1980 Everton-Liverpool 'derby'.

20 PLAYERS' NICKNAMES

The Flying Pig (Tommy Lawrence)
The Lawman (Denis Law)
Digger (John Barnes)
The Vulture (Emilio Butragueno)
Butch (Ray Wilkins)
Budgie (Johnny Byrne)
Sniffer (Allan Clarke)
Der Bomber (Gerd Muller)
Der Kaiser (Franz Beckenbauer)
The Cat (Peter Bonetti)
Crazy Horse (Emlyn Hughes)
Chopper (Ron Harris)
The Shark (Joe Jordan)
Bites Yer Legs (Norman Hunter)
The Rumble of Thunder (Luigi Riva)
Little Bird (Garrincha)
The Gentle Giant (John Charles)
Mighty Mouse (Kevin Keegan)
The Black Panther (Eusebio)
The Giraffe (Jack Charlton)

Former West Ham and England centre-forward Johnny Byrne was nicknamed Budgie because he never stopped talking. An irrepressible character, he nearly landed Greavsie and the England party in hot water on a 1964 tour of South America. As Brazil went down 3-0 in a violent clash with arch rivals Argentina in Sao Paulo, Budgie, who was watching with the rest of the England boys from a touchline bench, suddenly turned round and started conducting the partisan Brazilian fans in a chorus of 'Three-nil, Three-nil'. The next thing, fruit, cushions and stones were raining down on the England men. Alf Ramsey, feeling an apple splatter against his back, advised them to leg it fast and so they headed for the centre-circle. There they each grabbed the arm of a Brazilian player, ensuring a safe escort from the pitch. Budgie was not too popular after that incident.

MOST GOALS IN A GAME – ENGLAND AND SCOTLAND

1. John Petrie (Arbroath) v Bon Accord,
   Scottish Cup 1885   13
2. Gerry Baker (St Mirren) v Glasgow Univ.
   Scottish Cup 1960   10
   Alisdair D'Arcy (Dundee Harp) v Aberdeen Rovers,
   Scottish Cup 1885   10
   Joe Payne (Luton Town) v Bristol Rovers,
   D3 S 1936   10
5 Joe Baker (Hibernian) v Peebles Rovers,
   Scottish Cup 1961   9
   Bunny Bell (Tranmere Rovers) v Oldham Athletic,
   D3 N 1935   9
   Ted MacDougall (Bournemouth) v Margate,
   FA Cup 1971   9

Of course, these are only for senior games. There are countless tales of goalscoring feats in amateur football. Paul Moulden, who went on to play for Manchester City, netted an amazing 289 goals in 40 games for Bolton Lads Club in Bolton Boys' Federation Intermediate League and Cup matches during 1981-82. Women's soccer has had its moments too. In 1983, Linda Curl of Norwich Ladies scored no fewer than 22 goals in a 40-0 annihilation of Milton Keynes Reserves. Probably the unluckiest highscorer in history was St Albans City's Billy Minter who scored seven goals against Dulwich Hamlet in a 1922 FA Cup fourth qualifying round tie. Yet he still ended up on the losing side, as Dulwich won 8-7. Sometimes a spot of lenient refereeing can help goalscorers although in Yugoslavia, they once went a bit too far. In 1979, Illinden FC needed a big victory from their final match to boost their goal difference and thereby win promotion. Somehow they managed to persuade their opponents, Mladost, and the referee to help them out, with the result that Illinden emerged victorious 134-1. Presumably the goal against was to make it look genuine. They might have got away with it too had their promotion rivals not practised similar skullduggery, arranging their match to finish 88-0.

MOST WEMBLEY FA CUP FINALS

Five players have appeared in five FA Cup finals at
Wembley:

Joe Hulme	(Arsenal) 1927(L), 1930(W), 1932(L), 1936(W) (Huddersfield Town) 1938(L)
Johnny Giles	(Manchester United) 1963(W) (Leeds United) 1965(L), 1970(D), 1972(W), 1973(L)
Pat Rice	(Arsenal) 1971(W), 1972(L), 1978(L), 1979(W), 1980(L)
Frank Stapleton	(Arsenal) 1978(L), 1979(W), 1980(L) (Manchester United) 1983(W), 1985(W)
Ray Clemence	(Liverpool) 1971(L), 1974(W), 1977(L) (Tottenham Hotspur) 1982(W), 1987(L)

Johnny Giles' 1970 appearance for Leeds against Chelsea ended
in a draw at Wembley but the Londoners won the replay at Old
Trafford. However, taking FA Cup finals as a whole, none of these
can compete with the worthy Lord Kinnaird who appeared in a
record nine finals. He picked up five winners' medals – three with
Wanderers (1873, 1877 and 1878) and two with Old Etonians (1879
and 1882). The remarkable Jimmy Delaney actually appeared in
Cup finals in four different countries. He picked up winners' medals
with Celtic in the Scottish Cup (1937), Manchester United in the FA
Cup (1948), and Derry City in the Irish Cup (1954), and a losers'
medal when Cork Athletic lost to Shamrock Rovers in the 1956 FA of
Ireland Cup final.

10 CRICKETING FOOTBALLERS

Chris Balderstone (Leicestershire and Carlisle United)
Ian Botham (Somerset and Scunthorpe United)
Raich Carter (Derbyshire and Derby County)
Brian Close (Yorkshire and Arsenal)
Denis Compton (Middlesex and Arsenal)
Geoff Hurst (Essex and West Ham United)
Gary Lineker (Leicestershire and Leicester City)
Phil Neale (Worcestershire and Lincoln City)
Steve Ogrizovic (Shropshire and Coventry City)
Jim Standen (Worcestershire and Arsenal)

C ricketing footballers used to be commonplace but the demands of soccer today mean that they are now few and far between. Lincoln's Phil Neale was just about the last person to play both sports full-time. Even so, there's nothing like a moment of cricketing glory to recount to your football team-mates when you meet up for the start of a new season. Coventry goalkeeper Steve Ogrizovic certainly has plenty to crow about. Playing for Shropshire in the Nat-West Trophy against Somerset, he once clean bowled the great Viv Richards.

MOST FOOTBALL LEAGUE
APPEARANCES WITH ONE CLUB

1. John Trollope (Swindon Town, 1960-80)   770
2. Jimmy Dickinson (Portsmouth, 1946-65)   764
3. Roy Sproson (Port Vale, 1950-72)   761
4. Terry Paine (Southampton, 1956-74)   713
5. Billy Bonds (West Ham United, 1967-88)   663
6. Ron Harris (Chelsea, 1962-80)   655
   Steve Perryman (Tottenham Hotspur, 1969-86)   655
8. Ian Callaghan (Liverpool, 1960-78)   640
9. Jack Charlton (Leeds United, 1953-73)   629
   Joe Shaw (Sheffield United, 1948-66)   629

As well as being a great winger, Ian Callaghan was a model professional. He never stepped out of line, on or off the field, although I remember once when he managed to incur the wrath of Bill Shankly. We were on a European trip to Belgium and stayed out to have a few drinks too many. When we lurched back to the hotel, it was way past Shanks's curfew. He launched into us in typical fashion – something most of us were used to. But he was shocked to find little Ian among the sinners. As Ian stood swaying in the doorway, Shanks rounded on him last of all. 'And as for you Callaghan…you of all people…I'm going to tell your wife on you!' There are a few hard men in this list too. Tottenham's Stevie Perryman could look after himself while Ron 'Chopper' Harris was always a formidable opponent. Some players reckoned he was such a good butcher he should have worked at Sainsbury's! And Billy Bonds used to act as Trevor Brooking's 'minder' at West Ham. If anyone was giving Trevor a hard time on the pitch, he'd have a word with 'Bonzo' who would promptly sort them out. For the rest of the game, Trevor would have the freedom of midfield to display his silky skills without fear of getting a size 11 boot where it hurts.

MOST LEAGUE GOALS WITH ONE CLUB – ENGLAND AND SCOTLAND

1. Jimmy McGrory (Celtic, 1922-23, 1924-38)   397
2. Dixie Dean (Everton, 1925-37)   349
3. George Camsell (Middlesbrough, 1925-39)   326
4. John Atyeo (Bristol City, 1951-66)   315
5. Vic Watson (West Ham United, 1920-35)   306
6. Steve Bloomer (Derby County, 1892-1906, 1910-14) 291
7. Arthur Chandler (Leicester City, 1923-35)   259
8. Nat Lofthouse (Bolton Wanderers, 1946-61)   255
9. Arthur Rowley (Leicester City, 1950-58)   251
10. Joe Bradford (Birmingham City, 1920-35)   249

Nat Lofthouse, the old Lion of Vienna, was one of the most fearsome centre-forwards of the Fifties. As any goalkeeper will testify, notably Manchester United's Harry Gregg in the 1958 FA Cup final, he was a tough opponent. But Nat sometimes found himself on the receiving end too. He said that in his heyday, there were plenty of fellers who would kick your bollocks off. But he reckoned the difference between then and now was that at the end, they'd shake your hand and help you look for them.

MOST SCOTTISH LEAGUE GOALS IN A SEASON

1. Jimmy Smith (Ayr United, 1927-28)   66
2. Allan Mc Graw (Morton, 1963-64)   58
3. Bobby Skinner (Dunfermline, 1925-26)   53
4. Hugh Baird (Airdrieonians, 1954-55)   52
    Bill Mc Fadyen (Motherwell, 1931-32)   52

THE THINGS THEY SAY

'Football's a game of skill...we kicked them a bit and they kicked us a bit.' – Graham Roberts

'That Cookie. When he sold you a dummy, you had to pay to get back into the ground.' – Jim Baxter on fellow Scot Charlie Cooke

'Most dangerous opponent: My ex-wife.' – Frank Worthington in magazine questionnaire

'Claim to fame outside soccer: I once put together an MFI wardrobe in less than four days.' – Coventry striker Terry Gibson, answering another magazine

'It's like going to a different country.' – Ian Rush talking about playing in Italy

'And they were lucky to get nil.' – Len Shackleton, after scoring six for Newcastle in a 13-0 trouncing of Newport

'Blimey, the ground looks a bit different to Watford. Where's the dog track?' – Luther Blissett on his first visit to Milan's San Siro Stadium

'I want to be respected. I'd like to be like Trevor Brooking.' – Vinny Jones

'Too interested in sport. You will never make a living playing football.' – Gary Lineker's final school report

CHAPTER SIX

THE MANAGEMENT

MOST SUCCESSFUL FOOTBALL LEAGUE MANAGERS SINCE THE WAR

		Major trophies won
1.	Bob Paisley (Liverpool)	14
2.	Brian Clough (Derby/Nottingham Forest)	12
3.	Matt Busby (Manchester United)	8
	Bill Nicholson (Tottenham Hotspur)	8
5.	Don Revie (Leeds United)	7
	Bill Shankly (Liverpool)	7
7.	Stan Cullis (Wolverhampton Wanderers)	5
	Kenny Dalglish (Liverpool)	5
	Ron Saunders (Norwich City/Aston Villa)	5

When Bob Paisley was trainer under Shanks in the Sixties, they were quite a double act. Shanks was a great one for new inventions and so when he heard about a much-vaunted German black box, which was to revolutionize the treatment of injuries, he couldn't wait to try one out at Anfield. Every experiment needs a guinea pig, and little Jimmy Melia duly got on the treatment table and unveiled his injured knee for healing. The assembled pressmen watched expectantly. Bob attached the pads to Jimmy's leg and tried to read the instructions which were in German. He assured the increasingly agitated Shanks that he understood them perfectly – 'I was in Germany during the War...' Finally, Bob had everything wired up and told Jimmy to turn the dial. Nothing happened. Bob asked him to have another go, to turn it on full. Still nothing. Then Bob spotted the problem – the plug in the wall hadn't been switched on. Bob lent over and flicked the switch, at which point Jimmy, still with the dial at full, nearly hit the ceiling as the current surged through his leg! We all fell about laughing while Jimmy limped around the room screaming, 'I've been electrocuted'. It took a while before Bob lived that one down. Bob went on to become a great manager yet in terms of trophies won since the war, he still had a long way to go to catch up with Jock Stein who with Dunfermline and, of course primarily, Celtic, collected no fewer than 24, including that first coveted European Cup for Britain.

RECENT FOOTBALL LEAGUE FIRST DIVISION PLAYER-MANAGERS

(Up to end of 1991-92)

Les Allen	(Queen's Park Rangers, 1968-69)
Johnny Giles	(West Bromwich Albion, 1976-77)
Howard Kendall	(Everton, 1981-82)
Kenny Dalglish	(Liverpool, 1985-90)
Trevor Francis	(Queen's Park Rangers, 1988-89, Sheffield Wednesday, 1991-)
Terry Butcher	(Coventry City, 1990-91)
Peter Reid	(Manchester City, 1990-)

In my experience, it's hard enough being a manager without playing as well, particularly at the highest level. Graeme Souness discovered that in his spell up at Ibrox where he frequently fell foul of the referees, giving rise to the crack that they'd got a new drink in Glasgow called the Souness – one half and you're off.

FOOTBALL LEAGUE CLUBS WITH MOST MANAGERS SINCE THE WAR

(Up to the end of 1991-92)

1.	Stockport County	25
2.	Halifax Town	23
	Walsall	23
4.	Doncaster Rovers	22
	Torquay United	22
6.	Darlington	21
	Rochdale	21
8.	Bradford City	20
	Bury	20
	Carlisle United	20
	Grimsby Town	20
	Plymouth Argyle	20
13.	Birmingham City	19
	Crystal Palace	19
	Exeter City	19
	Hartlepool United	19
	West Bromwich Albion	19
18.	Manchester City	18
	Northampton Town	18
	Coventry City	18
20.	Blackburn Rovers	17
	Blackpool	17
	Brentford	17
	Crewe Alexandra	17
	Mansfield Town	17
	Preston North End	17
	Scunthorpe United	17
	Watford	17

When Torquay appointed Paul Compton in May, he was the club's fifth manager in 18 months. But that's nothing compared with former League members Southport who, in the Northern Premier League in 1983, had four managers in two weeks. Having sacked Russ Perkins on the Saturday, they tried to persuade John King to take over. King provisionally accepted the post on the Tuesday but changed his mind two days later. The following Sunday, Bob Murphy took on the challenge, only to resign on the Thursday. Finally on the Saturday, exactly a fortnight after Perkins' departure, Alex Gibson became Southport's manager. He lasted two months.

SHORTEST MANAGERIAL REIGNS

1. Bill Lambton (Scunthorpe United, 1959)   3 days
2. Steve Murray (Forfar Athletic, 1980)   5 days
3. Tim Ward (Exeter City, 1953)   7 days
4. Johnny Cochrane (Reading, 1939)   13 days
5. Jimmy McIlroy (Bolton Wanderers, 1970)   16 days

Bill Lambton may only have been in charge of Scunthorpe for three days but he had time to see his team play. Alas, they lost 3-0 to Liverpool at Anfield in a Second Division match. But that wasn't the reason for his departure. Nor were poor results the cause of Tim Ward's exit. Having joined Exeter as manager, he was suddenly recalled to action by Barnsley who still held his registration as a player.

FOOTBALL LEAGUE CLUBS WITH FEWEST MANAGERS SINCE THE WAR

(Up to the end of 1991-92, not including clubs who have joined since 1970)

1.	West Ham United	6
2.	Nottingham Forest	7
	Southampton	7
4.	Ipswich Town	8
	Liverpool	8
	Manchester United	8
7.	Arsenal	9
	Barnsley	9
9.	Oxford United	10
10.	Everton	11
	Gillingham	11
	Reading	11
	Stoke City	11
	Tottenham Hotspur	11
15.	Bristol City	12
	Charlton Athletic	12
	Chester City	12
	Chesterfield	12
	Derby County	12
	Tranmere Rovers	12

In fact, Billy Bonds is only the seventh West Ham manager this century, following in the footsteps of Syd King (1900-31), Charlie Paynter (1931-50), Ted Fenton (1950-61), Ron Greenwood (1961-74), John Lyall (1974-89) and Lou Macari (1989-90). It's a shame that last season the controversial bond scheme rather tarnished their reputation as a friendly club.

DOUBLE CHAMPIONS

The following Football League managers have played in and managed Championship-winning teams:

Ted Drake   Player: Arsenal 1934, 1935, 1938
                     Manager: Chelsea 1955

Bill Nicholson   Player: Tottenham Hotspur 1951
                     Manager: Tottenham Hotspur 1961

Alf Ramsey   Player: Tottenham Hotspur 1951
                     Manager: Ipswich Town 1962

Joe Mercer   Player: Everton 1939, Arsenal 1948, 1953
                     Manager: Manchester City 1968

Dave Mackay   Player: Tottenham Hotspur 1961
                     Manager: Derby County 1975

Bob Paisley   Player: Liverpool 1947
                     Manager: Liverpool 1976, 1977, 1979,
                                  1980, 1982, 1983

Howard Kendall   Player: Everton 1970
                     Manager: Everton 1985, 1987

Kenny Dalglish   Player: Liverpool 1979, 1980, 1982, 1983,
                                  1984
                     Player-Manager: Liverpool 1986, 1988,
                                  1990

George Graham   Player: Arsenal 1971
                     Manager: Arsenal 1989, 1991

Like a lot of the 'old school', the late Joe Mercer had trouble pronouncing continental players' names. When Joe said them, regardless of whether they were Spanish, Polish or French, they all came out sounding like 'Beethoven'. Once waxing lyrical about the Holland team of the Seventies, he said on television: 'That number 14 for Holland is a marvellous player...that Johan Strauss.' Great stuff. Scotland's Willie Ormond was another – he often used to avoid discussing opposition players because he couldn't pronounce their names. But on one occasion, he did warn his players: 'Watch out for the blond at corners and free-kicks.' The trouble was there were six big blonds in the other team. Scotland were playing Sweden!

LONGEST-SERVING CURRENT FOOTBALL LEAGUE MANAGERS

(up to May 1992)

		Years	Months
1.	Brian Clough (Nottingham Forest)	17	4
2.	Joe Royle (Oldham Athletic)	9	10
3.	Dario Gradi (Crewe Alexandra)	8	11
4.	John Rudge (Port Vale)	8	5
5.	Arthur Cox (Derby County)	8	0
6.	Steve Coppell (Crystal Palace)	7	11
7.	Harry McNally (Chester City)	6	11
8.	George Graham (Arsenal)	6	0
9.	Barry Fry (Barnet)	5	10
10.	Graham Turner (Wolverhampton Wanderers)	5	7

As one wag put it, Cloughie's record speaks for itself – if only it could get a word in. But he never has made it as manager of a national team even though when the Irish job was vacant, he reckoned it would be an easy trip for him from Nottingham – just a straight walk across the Irish Sea. Still, he's done a fabulous job with Forest and has kept us entertained on and off the pitch. Nevertheless, someone has been in the hot seat longer than Cloughie. For up in Scotland, Jim McLean has been boss of Dundee United since 1971. Jim is also the club chairman which presumably means he doesn't have to worry too much about getting the dreaded vote of confidence. Not that he'd have anything to worry about – in those 21 years Jim has taken United from being very much the second team in Dundee to becoming a major force in Europe.

MOST MANAGER OF THE MONTH AWARDS

(this includes Manager of the Month, Divisional Manager of the Month, Manager of the Year, Divisional Manager of the Season, Special Awards and the League Managers' Association Barclay's Achievement Award)

1. Brian Clough (Derby Co., Nottm Forest) 24
2. Bob Paisley (Liverpool) 22
3. Graham Taylor (Lincoln City, Watford, Aston Villa) 21
4. Ron Atkinson (Cambridge United, West Brom,
     Man United, Sheffield Wednesday 15
     Dave Smith (Mansfield Town, Southend United,
     Plymouth Argyle, Torquay United 15
     Jim Smith (Colchester United, Blackburn Rovers,
     Birmingham City, Oxford United, QPR,
     Newcastle United 15
7. Ron Saunders (Norwich City, Aston Villa,
     Birmingham City) 14
8. Kenny Dalglish (Liverpool) 13
     John Lyall (West Ham United, Ipswich Town) 13
10. Dave Bassett (Wimbledon, Sheffield United) 12
     George Graham (Millwall, Arsenal) 12
     Howard Kendall (Blackburn Rovers, Everton) 12
13. Terry Venables (Crystal Palace, QPR, Barcelona) 11*
14. Don Revie (Leeds United) 10
15. Lawrie McMenemy (Grimsby Town, Southampton) 9
     Bobby Robson (Ipswich Town) 9
     Howard Wilkinson (Sheffield Wednesday, Leeds
     United) 9
18. Alex Ferguson (Aberdeen, Manchester United) 8
     Graham Turner (Shrewsbury Town, Wolves) 8
20. Bill Shankly (Liverpool) 7
     Jimmy Sirrel (Notts County) 7

* Terry Venables total includes four awards in Spain

The awards began as recently as 1969 which explains the abscence of the likes of Matt Busby and Bill Nicholson and probably accounts for why Shanks only received seven. Although Shanks had the greatest respect for his fellow managers – he particularly admired Jock Stein – I doubt whether he would have wanted to have come second to any of them. He had to be a winner through and through – even in six-a-side practice matches. Shanks hated losing them and would frequently swap sides half-way through just so that he could end up on the winning team. Right at the end of one game, with the scores level, a disputed goal was awarded against a Shanks' team which included Chris Lawler, one of the quiet men of Anfield. Everyone was convinced it was a goal except Shanks. He protested vehemently before, in desperation, announcing: 'All right, we'll bring in a man whose integrity is never in doubt. A man of few words who'll tell the truth – Chrissie Lawler. Now Chris, son, your honest opinion…was the ball over the line?' 'It was a goal, boss,' replied Chris. Shanks was beside himself. 'Can you believe that? I've waited ten years for the man to open his mouth and the first thing he tells me is a lie!'

CUP DOUBLES

The following managers have all played in and managed
FA Cup winning teams:

Peter McWilliam	Player: Newcastle United 1910
	Manager: Tottenham Hotspur 1921
Billy Walker	Player: Aston Villa 1920
	Manager: Sheffield Wednesday 1935,
	Nottingham Forest 1959
Jimmy Seed	Player: Tottenham Hotspur 1921
	Manager: Charlton Athletic 1947
Matt Busby	Player: Manchester City 1934
	Manager: Manchester United 1948, 1963
Joe Smith	Player: Bolton Wanderers 1923, 1926
	Manager: Blackpool 1953
Bill Shankly	Player: Preston North End 1938
	Manager: Liverpool 1965, 1974
Joe Mercer	Player: Arsenal 1950
	Manager: Manchester City 1969
Don Revie	Player: Manchester City 1956
	Manager: Leeds United 1972
Bob Stokoe	Player: Newcastle United 1955
	Manager: Sunderland 1973
Kenny Dalglish	Player-Manager: Liverpool 1986
	Manager: Liverpool 1989
Terry Venables	Player: Tottenham Hotspur 1967
	Manager: Tottenham Hotspur 1991

After gaining two Cup winners' medals playing for Bolton, Joe Smith returned to Wembley as a manager with Blackpool in 1953 and saw his team emerge triumphant from the memorable Matthews final...at the expense of Bolton. Stanley Matthews was at his brilliant best that day. Throughout his career, his accuracy was unbelievable – his old England forward partner, Tommy Lawton, reckoned that Matthews was so perfect with crosses that he could land the ball on his centre-parting.

LONGEST POST-WAR FOOTBALL LEAGUE MANAGERIAL REIGNS

		years
1.	Matt Busby (Manchester United, 1945-69)	24
2.	Ted Bates (Southampton, 1955-73)	18
	Bert Tann (Bristol Rovers, 1950-68)	18
4.	Brian Clough (Nottingham Forest, 1975-)	17
	Bill Ridding (Bolton Wanderers, 1951-68)	17
	Tony Waddington (Stoke City, 1960-77)	17
7.	Stan Cullis (Wolverhampton Wanderers, 1948-64)	16
	Bill Nicholson (Tottenham Hotspur, 1958-74)	16
9.	John Lyall (West Ham United, 1974-89)	15
	Bill Shankly (Liverpool, 1959-74)	15

Before taking the Manchester United job in 1945, Matt Busby turned down the post as coach at Anfield. I wonder how history would have changed had he accepted. In the Sixties there was always a keen but friendly rivalry between Shanks and his opposite number at Everton, Harry Catterick, who himself served at Goodison Park for 12 years. After signing big Ron Yeats, Shanks boasted to Harry Catterick that with him at centre-half, he could afford to play Arthur Askey in goal! And Shanks used to love to tell the story of how when Everton reached the Cup final in 1966, Princess Margaret asked their captain Brian Labone exactly where Everton was. When he replied that it was in Liverpool, HRH, according to Shanks, said: 'Of course, we had your first team here last year.' Knowing Shanks, I bet he even convinced himself that the story was true.

LONGEST FOOTBALL LEAGUE MANAGERIAL REIGNS IN HISTORY

		years
1.	Fred Everiss (West Bromwich Albion, 1902-48)	46
2.	George Ramsay (Aston Villa, 1884-1926)	42
3.	John Addenbrooke (Wolverhampton Wanderers, 1885-1922)	37
4.	Frank Watt (Newcastle United, 1895-1930)	35
5.	John Nicholson (Sheffield United, 1899-1932)	33
6.	Sam Allen (Swindon Town, 1902-33)	31
7.	Syd King (West Ham United, 1902-32)	30
8.	Bob Jack (Plymouth Argyle, 1910-38)	28
	Charles Webb (Brighton & Hove Albion, 1919-47)	28
10.	Charlie Green (Luton Town, 1901-28)	27
11.	David Calderhead (Chelsea, 1907-33)	26
12.	Charles Foweraker (Bolton Wanderers, 1919-44)	25
13.	Matt Busby (Manchester United, 1945-69)	24
14.	Harry Curtis (Brentford, 1926-49)	23
	Bob Kyle (Sunderland, 1905-28)	23
	Jimmy Seed (Charlton Athletic, 1933-56)	23
	Joe Smith (Blackpool, 1935-58)	23

Along with Bill Nicholson, Bolton's Charles Foweraker is the only man to have managed three FA Cup winning teams. Foweraker's triumphant visits to Wembley were in 1923, 1926 and 1929. In common with a number of managers in the early years, Fred Everiss acted as secretary/manager at West Brom. Part of his job was to make sure that the players were allocated tickets for away games. Once for the 'derby' at Villa Park, the tickets were late arriving and Albion's England international, Jesse Pennington, was refused admission to the ground by a stubborn gate-man. There were 30,000 people inside but the captain of the visiting team was locked out! Finally in the nick of time, Jesse gained admission. And he had the last laugh – Albion won.

10 MANAGERS' QUOTES

'My chairman Robert Maxwell, they ought to let him run football.' – Jim Smith, when manager of Oxford United

'Once he starts to open his legs, you've got a problem.' –Howard Wilkinson about speedy Villa winger Tony Daley

'Even when you're dead, you shouldn't lie down and let yourself be buried.' – Former Everton boss Gordon Lee

'I felt a lump in my mouth as the ball went in.' – Terry Venables, reflecting on a goal conceded

'He can't run, can't tackle and can't head a ball. The only time he goes forward is to toss the coin.' – Tommy Docherty talking about Ray Wilkins

'Obviously for Scunthorpe, it would be a nice scalp to put Wimbledon on their bottoms.' – Dave Bassett

'There are three types of Oxo cubes. Light brown for chicken stock, dark brown for beef stock, and light blue for laughing stock.' – Tommy Docherty on Manchester City's 1988 struggles

'He did a lot of growing up in Hong Kong.' – Graeme Souness, then manager at Rangers, on 5 ft 4 in. striker John Spencer, back at Ibrox after a year playing in the Far East

'They offered me a handshake of £10,000 to settle amicably. I told them they would have to be a lot more amicable than that.' – Tommy Docherty after losing the Preston job in 1981

'Devon Loch was a better finisher.' – Ron Atkinson on Aston Villa's goal famine

CHAPTER SEVEN

NON-LEAGUE

RECORD TRANSFERS FROM NON-LEAGUE TO FOOTBALL LEAGUE

1. Andrew Clarke (Barnet to Wimbledon, 1991) £250,000
2. Phil Gridelet (Barnet to Barnsley, 1990) £175,000
3. Andy Hunt (Kettering to Newcastle United, 1988) £150,000
4. Robert Codner (Barnet to Brighton, 1988) £125,000
    Nicky Bissett (Barnet to Brighton, 1988) £125,000
6. Peter Guthrie (Weymouth to Tottenham Hotspur, 1988) £100,000
    Stan Collymore (Stafford Rgrs to Crystal Palace, 1991) £100,000
8. Ian Woan (Runcorn to Nottingham Forest, 1989) £80,000
9. Iain Dowie (Hendon to Luton Town, 1988) £75,000
10. Andy Hessenthaler (Redbridge Forest to Watford, 1991) £65,000

FIRST 10 TRANSFERS FROM NON-LEAGUE OF OVER £20,000

1. Garry Birtles (Long Eaton Utd to Nottingham Forest) 1976
2. John Barton (Worcester City to Everton) 1978
3. Tony Cunningham (Stourbridge to Lincoln City) 1979
    Eamon O'Keefe (Mossley to Everton) 1979
    Trevor Peake (Nuneaton Borough to Lincoln City) 1979
    Kevin Wilson (Banbury United to Derby County) 1979

7.	Kerry Dixon (Dunstable Town to Reading)	1980
	Tim Smithers (Nuneaton Borough to Oxford United)	1980
	David Wiffill (Bath City to Manchester City)	1980
10.	Trevor Senior (Dorchester Town to Portsmouth)	1981

10 MORE FORMER NON-LEAGUERS WHO HAVE MADE IT TO THE TOP

	Non-League club
Tony Agana (Notts County)	Weymouth
Brett Angell (Southend United)	Cheltenham Town
Gary Crosby (Nottingham Forest)	Grantham
Jason Dodd (Southampton)	Bath City
Mike Lake (Sheffield United)	Macclesfield Town
Stuart Pearce (Nottingham Forest)	Wealdstone
Alan Smith (Arsenal)	Alvechurch
Shaun Teale (Aston Villa)	Weymouth
Mark Ward (Everton)	Northwich Victoria
Eric Young (Crystal Palace)	Slough Town

These three lists just show what bargains there are to be had in non-league football which, thanks to the pyramid system among the lower leagues, is currently stronger than ever. And there are many more success stories besides those mentioned above. Manchester United's Gary Pallister used to play for Northern Leaguers Billingham; Manchester City keeper Tony Coton learnt his trade with West Midlands club Mile Oak; Andy Comyn, a stalwart of the Derby defence last season, started out, like Alan Smith, with little Alvechurch; Ken Charlery, whose goals earned Peterborough promotion, was once with Fisher Athletic; and Nicky Tanner, who settled in to the heart of the Liverpool defence, began his career with west country minnows Mangotsfield. It all goes to explain why at many non-league grounds these days, there are more scouts than at a jamboree.

30 NON-LEAGUE NICKNAMES

The Yeltz (Halesowen Town)
The Ducks (Aylesbury United)
The Choirboys (Wycombe Wanderers)
Nuts and Bolts (Ashford Town)
The Bloods (Saffron Walden Town)
Over the Bridge (Abingdon Town)
The Cardinals (Woking)
The Terras (Weymouth)
The Gladiators (Matlock Town)
The Russians (Rushden)
The Rocks (Bognor Regis Town)
The Sandgrounders (Southport)
The Martyrs (Merthyr Tydfil)
The Dinc (Yeading)
The Glassboys (Stourbridge)
The Gingerbreads (Grantham Town)
The Dragons (Wivenhoe Town)
The Silkmen (Macclesfield Town)
The Chicks (Dorking Town)
The Beavers (Hampton)
The Pilgrims (Boston United)
The Glovers (Yeovil Town)
The Curlews (Chertsey Town)
The Dolphins (Poole Town)
The Badgers (Eastwood Town)
The Bears (Congleton Town)
The Adders (Atherstone United)
The Moles (Molesey)
The Linnets (Kings Lynn)
Gat (Margate)

Some great nicknames here, but my favourite is that of Worthing who are known as The Rebels. If you've ever been to Worthing, you'll know it's just about the least rebellious place on earth. You're more likely to be mown down by a bath chair than a Harley-Davidson.

THE 10 HIGHEST ALLIANCE AND CONFERENCE GATES

1.	Lincoln City v Wycombe Wanderers, 1988	9,432
2.	Lincoln City v Boston United, 1988	7,542
3.	Colchester United v Altrincham, 1991	7,221
4.	Colchester United v Barrow, 1992	7,193
5.	Colchester United v Kettering Town, 1992	6,303
6.	Wycombe Wanderers v Witton Albion, 1992	6,035
7.	Barnet v Darlington, 1990	5,880
8.	Boston United v Lincoln City, 1987	5,822
9.	Scarborough v Weymouth, 1987	5,640
10.	Darlington v Cheltenham Town, 1990	5,525

THE 15 OLDEST MAJOR NON-LEAGUE CLUBS

1.	Worksop Town	1861
2.	Hitchin Town	1865
3.	Droylsden	1866
4.	Harefield United	1868
5.	Maidenhead United	1869
6.	Marlow	1870
7.	Southall	1871
	Uxbridge	1871
9.	Bury Town	1872
	Saffron Walden Town	1872
11.	Gainsborough Trinity	1873
	Halesowen Town	1873
	Macclesfield Town	1873
14.	Bishop's Stortford	1874
	Northwich Victoria	1874

In company with Maidenhead, Marlow are the only club to have entered every single FA Cup since the inaugural competition in 1871-72. It is not known whether any of their players can boast a similar achievement...

THE 15 YOUNGEST MAJOR NON-LEAGUE CLUBS

1.	Dagenham and Redbridge	1992
2.	Purfleet	1985
3.	Knowsley United	1984
4.	Dover Athletic	1983
5.	Atherstone United	1979
6.	Fleetwood Town	1977
7.	Frickley Athletic	1976
	Stevenage Borough	1976
9.	Waltham Forest	1975
10.	Wivenhoe Town	1974
11.	Camberley Town	1969
12.	Farnborough Town	1967
	Malden Vale	1967
14.	Irlam Town	1965
	Yeading	1965

Redbridge Forest were formed by the amalgamation of that famous old club, Walthamstow Avenue, and Leytonstone-Ilford, who were themselves a 1979 amalgamation of Leytonstone and Ilford. Then in the summer they joined forces with Dagenham and are now known as Dagenham and Redbridge. In fact, they seem to have had more unions than Zsa Zsa Gabor. And what tremendous progress Farnborough Town have made. Only founded 25 years ago, they gave West Ham the fright of their lives in last season's FA Cup.

MOST FA AMATEUR CUP WINS

1.	Bishop Auckland	10
2.	Clapton	5
	Crook Town	5
4.	Dulwich Hamlet	4
5.	Bromley	3
	Hendon	3
	Leytonstone	3
8.	Ilford	2
	Leyton	2
	Middlesbrough	2
	Old Carthusians	2
	Pegasus	2
	Walthamstow Avenue	2

Eighty-one clubs entered the first FA Amateur Cup in 1893-94, among them Reading, Berwick Rangers, Ipswich, Tottenham Hotspur, Middlesbrough, Shrewsbury, New Brompton (who later became Gillingham), Colchester and West Herts (now known as Watford). The winners were Old Carthusians and not all of today's professional clubs fared too well. Ipswich were bundled out 1-0 by Ilford while Spurs were suspended for infringing the amateur rules and so Clapham Rovers received a bye at their expense. The Amateur Cup's finest years were probably the early Fifties when the might of Bishop Auckland was challenged by the student team Pegasus. Did you know that Bob Paisley won an Amateur Cup winner's medal with Bishop Auckland in 1939? The competition was discontinued in 1974 but among its winners were Middlesbrough (1894-95), Barnet (1945-46) and Wimbledon (1962-63).

PLAYERS WITH MOST ENGLAND AMATEUR CAPS (POST-WAR)

1. Rod Haider (Kingstonian, Hendon)   65
2. John Swannell (Hendon)   61
3. Mike Pinner (Cambridge University, Pegasus,
      QPR, RAF, Hendon, Leyton Orient)   52
4. Ted Powell (Sutton United, Wycombe Wanderers,
      Kingstonian)   51
5. Jim Lewis (Walthamstow Avenue, Chelsea)   49
   Larry Pritchard (Sutton United, Wycombe Wdrs)   48
7. Roger Day (Enfield, Slough Town, Ilford)   43
   Kenny Gray (Leytonstone, Enfield)   43
9. Peter Deadman (Barking, Hendon)   40
10. Laurie Topp (Hendon)   32
    Charlie Townsend (Wealdstone)   32

CLUBS WHO PRODUCED MOST ENGLAND AMATEUR INTERNATIONALS (POST-WAR)

1. Enfield   24
2. Bishop Auckland   18
   Leytonstone   18
4. Hendon   15
5. Pegasus   13
   Sutton United   13
   Walthamstow Avenue   13
8. Barnet   11
   Crook Town   11
   Wycombe Wanderers   11

CLUBS WHO HAVE APPEARED IN MOST FA TROPHY FINALS

1.	Telford United	5
2.	Scarborough	4
3.	Altrincham	3
	Stafford Rangers	3
5.	Dagenham	2
	Enfield	2
	Kidderminster Harriers	2
	Macclesfield Town	2
	Northwich Victoria	2

Telford and Scarborough lead the way with three wins apiece. The goalkeeper in Stafford Rangers' successful 1972 team was Milija Aleksic who went on to win an FA Cup winners' medal with Spurs in 1981. The only other player to taste FA Trophy and FA Cup victories is John Radford, with Arsenal in 1971 and Bishop's Stortford ten years later.

---

10 NON-LEAGUE GROUNDS

Old Spotted Dog Ground (Clapton)
The Dripping Pan (Lewes)
Butchers Arms (Droylsden)
The Dovecote (Shepshed Charterhouse)
Throstle Nest (Farsley Celtic)
Giant Axe (Lancaster City)
The Oval (Eastbourne United)
Gander Green Lane (Sutton United)
Crabble Athletic Ground (Dover Athletic)
Sheepy Road Ground (Atherstone United)

12 FORMER INTERNATIONALS WHO WENT INTO NON-LEAGUE FOOTBALL

Peter Barnes (England) – Northwich Victoria
Willie Carr (Scotland) – Worcester City
Martin Chivers (England) – Barnet
Gerry Daly (Eire) – Telford United
Andy Gray (Scotland) – Cheltenham Town
Frank Gray (Scotland) – Darlington
Gordon Hill (England) – Northwich Victoria, Stafford
    Rangers
Alan Kennedy (England) – Northwich Victoria
Mark Lawrenson (Eire) – Barnet
Derek Parlane (Scotland) – Macclesfield Town
Alex Stepney (England) – Altrincham

There are others too, including, of course, my sparring partner who spent his twilight years at Barnet. Million-pound man Steve Daley finished up at Kettering, Pop Robson joined Gateshead and little Georgie Armstrong turned out for Trowbridge. But I can't help wondering what the genteel locals of Cheltenham made of the battering-ram style of Andy Gray. It must have been like Rambo addressing a Women's Institute meeting.

CHAPTER EIGHT

THE WORLD GAME

TOP 10 CAPS – ENGLAND

(up to end of June 1992)

1.	Peter Shilton (1970-90)	125
2.	Bobby Moore (1962-73)	108
3.	Bobby Charlton (1958-70)	106
4.	Billy Wright (1946-59)	105
5.	Bryan Robson (1980-91)	90
6.	Kenny Sansom (1979-88)	86
7.	Ray Wilkins (1976-86)	84
8.	Gary Lineker (1984-92)	80
9.	Terry Butcher (1980-90)	77
10.	Tom Finney (1946-58)	76

The name at the foot of that list always meant a lot to Shanks. Tom Finney was his favourite player and of course they played together at Preston. He was always amazed at Finney's stamina – he reckoned the winger could have played in his overcoat and still run rings round most full-backs. Shanks knew how important Finney was to a team and how closely he had to be watched. As an opposing manager, he said he'd have had four men marking him during the pre-match kick-in!

TOP 10 CAPS – NORTHERN IRELAND

1. Pat Jennings (1964-86) 119
2. Sammy McIlroy (1972-87) 88
3. Mal Donaghy (1980-) 76
4. Jimmy Nicholl (1976-86) 73
5. David McCreery (1976-90) 67
6. Martin O'Neill (1972-85) 64
7. Gerry Armstrong (1977-86) 63
8. Terry Neill (1961-73) 59
9. Billy Bingham (1951-64) 56
   Danny Blanchflower (1950-63) 56

D anny Blanchflower was a great leader of men, both for club and country. I remember Greavsie telling me that before Spurs' 1961 European Cup Winners' Cup final with Atletico Madrid, the Tottenham boys had been feeling in awe of their opponents. Bill Nicholson had been going on about what great players Atletico had and it was starting to get to them. It was only when Danny chipped in that the Spaniards must be even more petrified about facing John White, Cliff Jones, Bobby Smith and co. that the mood in the dressing-room changed. Suddenly Spurs realised they were more than a match for anyone and went out and walloped Atletico 5-1 to become the first British team to win a European trophy.

TOP 10 CAPS – SCOTLAND

1. Kenny Dalglish (1972-87) 102
2. Alex McLeish (1980-91) 76
3. Willie Miller (1975-90) 65
4. Danny McGrain (1973-82) 62
5. Paul Mc Stay (1984-) 60
6. Richard Gough (1983-) 59
7. Jim Leighton (1983-90) 58
8. Roy Aitken (1980-90) 56
9. Denis Law (1959-74) 55
10. Billy Bremner (1965-76) 54
 Graeme Souness (1975-86) 54

TOP 10 CAPS – WALES

1. Peter Nicholas (1979-) 73
2. Joey Jones (1976-86) 72
3. Ivor Allchurch (1951-66) 68
4. Brian Flynn (1975-84) 66
5. Neville Southall (1982-) 61
6. Cliff Jones (1954-69) 59
 Terry Yorath (1970-81) 59
8. Leighton Phillips (1971-82) 58
 Kevin Ratcliffe (1981-) 58
10. Leighton James (1972-83) 54
 Ian Rush (1980-) 54

TOP 10 CAPS – REPUBLIC OF IRELAND

1. Liam Brady (1975-90)   72
2. Frank Stapleton (1977-90)   71
3. David O'Leary (1977-)   65
4. Kevin Moran (1980-91)   62
5. Johnny Giles (1960-79)   60
6. Pat Bonner (1981-)   57
   Mick McCarthy (1984-)   57
8. Don Givens (1969-82)   56
9. Chris Hughton (1980-)   54
   Paul McGrath (1985-)   54

TOP 10 GOALSCORERS – ENGLAND

1. Bobby Charlton (1958-70)   49
2. Gary Lineker (1985-92)   48
3. Jimmy Greaves (1959-67)   44
4. Tom Finney (1946-58)   30
   Nat Lofthouse (1950-58)   30
6. Vivian Woodward (1903-11)   29
7. Steve Bloomer (1895-1907)   28
8. Bryan Robson (1981-92)   26
9. Geoff Hurst (1966-71)   24
10. Stan Mortensen (1947-53)   23

Believe it or not, Stan Mortensen actually made his debut *against* England. He was named as one of the England reserves for a wartime international against Wales in 1943 but when Welsh wing-half Ivor Powell was carried off injured, England generously allowed Stan to go on and take his place. It was a painful experience though as Wales crashed 8-3. I bet Stan was glad to get back to being English.

TOP 10 GOALSCORERS – NORTHERN IRELAND

1.	Gerry Armstrong (1977-86)	12
	Joe Bambrick (1929-38)	12
	Colin Clarke (1986-)	12
	Billy Gillespie (1913-31)	12
5.	Billy Bingham (1951-64)	10
	Johnny Crossan (1960-68)	10
	Jimmy Mc Ilroy (1952-66)	10
	Peter Mc Parland (1954-62)	10
9.	George Best (1964-78)	9
	Olphie Stanfield (1887-97)	9
	Norman Whiteside (1982-90)	9

TOP 10 GOALSCORERS – SCOTLAND

1.	Kenny Dalglish (1972-87)	30
	Denis Law (1959-74)	30
3.	Hughie Gallacher (1924-35)	23
4.	Lawrie Reilly (1949-57)	22
5.	R.C. Hamilton (1899-1911)	14
	Mo Johnston (1984-)	14
7.	Bob McColl (1896-1908)	13
	Andrew Wilson (1920-23)	13
9.	Ally McCoist (1986-)	12
	John Smith (1877-84)	12
	Billy Steel (1947-53)	12

Hughie Gallacher's total was achieved in just 20 internationals – a phenomenal rate of scoring at this level.

TOP 10 GOALSCORERS – WALES

1. Ivor Allchurch (1951-66)   23
   Trevor Ford (1947-57)   23
3. Ian Rush (1980-)   20
4. John Charles (1950-65)   15
   Cliff Jones (1954-69)   15
6. John Toshack (1969-80)   13
7. Dai Astley (1931-39)   12
8. Billy Meredith (1895-1920)   11
9. Leighton James (1972-83)   10
   Bill Lewis (1885-98)   10
   Dean Saunders (1986-)   10

TOP 10 GOALSCORERS – REPUBLIC OF IRELAND

1. Frank Stapleton (1977-90)   20
2. Don Givens (1969-82)   19
3. Noel Cantwell (1954-67)   14
4. Gerry Daly (1973-87)   13
5. J. Dunne (1930-39)   12
6. Liam Brady (1975-90)   9
7. John Aldridge (1986-)   8
   Dermot Curtis (1957-64)   8
   Tony Grealish (1976-86)   8
   Niall Quinn (1986-)   8

J ack Charlton has done a terrific job with the Republic of Ireland. They always had good players but somehow were never able to find a winning team. He's put up with all the jokes – like if you have a fortnight's holiday in Dublin, you qualify for an international cap, and how the Irish players didn't know their national anthem from Albania's. And at last John Aldridge has started scoring a few goals after a nightmare start when he just couldn't find the net. It got so bad that at the end of his 19th goalless game for the Republic, one press wag commented: 'I see Aldridge has kept a clean sheet again.'

SHORTEST ENGLAND CAREERS

		Minutes
1.	Jimmy Barrett (West Ham United, 1928)	8
	Peter Ward (Brighton & Hove Albion, 1980)	8
3.	Brian Marwood (Arsenal, 1988)	9
4	Peter Davenport (Nottingham Forest, 1985)	17
5.	Kevin Hector (Derby County, 1973) (from 2 games)	18
6.	Brian Little (Aston Villa, 1975)	19
7.	Steve Perryman (Tottenham Hotspur, 1982)	20
8.	Nigel Winterburn (Arsenal, 1989)	23
9.	Trevor Whymark (Ipswich Town, 1977)	26
10.	Frank Hartley (Oxford City & Spurs, 1923)	4

C entre-half Jimmy Barrett had the misfortune to be injured shortly after making his debut against Northern Ireland and never played again for his country. Another one-cap wonder was W.H. Carr who turned out for 75 minutes against Scotland in 1875... after arriving late having missed the train. He was obviously never forgiven.

THE 10 OLDEST ENGLAND PLAYERS SINCE THE WAR

		Years	Days
1.	Stanley Matthews (Blackpool,1957)	42	103
2.	Peter Shilton (Derby County 1990)	40	292
3.	Leslie Compton (Arsenal, 1950)	38	71
4.	Tom Finney (Preston North End, 1958)	36	200
5.	Bert Williams (Wolves, 1955)	35	264
6.	Dave V Watson (Stoke City, 1982)	35	240
7.	Frank Swift (Manchester City, 1949)	35	145
8.	Billy Wright (Wolves, 1959)	35	111
9.	Ray Clemence (Tottenham Hotspur, 1983)	35	103
10.	Ted Ditchburn (Tottenham Hotspur, 1956)	35	42

THE 10 YOUNGEST ENGLAND PLAYERS SINCE THE WAR

		Years	Days
1.	Duncan Edwards (Manchester United, 1955)	18	183
2.	Jimmy Greaves (Chelsea, 1959)	19	86
3.	Joe Baker (Hibernian, 1959)	19	123
4	John Barnes (Watford, 1983)	19	222
5.	Ray Wilkins (Chelsea, 1976)	19	256
6.	Lee Sharpe (Manchester United, 1991)	19	304
7.	Nick Pickering (Sunderland, 1983)	19	309
8.	Tony Allen (Stoke City, 1959)	19	324
9.	Johnny Haynes (Fulham, 1954)	19	350
	Bobby Thomson (Wolves, 1963)	19	350

THE 10 OLDEST SCOTTISH INTERNATIONAL DEBUTANTS

		Years	Days
1.	Ronnie Simpson (Celtic, 1967)	36	186
2.	Thomas Pearson (Newcastle United, 1947)	34	27
3.	Jimmy Logie (Arsenal, 1952)	32	348
4.	Bill Summers (St Mirren, 1926)	32	277
5.	Peter Kerr (Hibernian, 1924)	32	255
6.	Donald Colman (Aberdeen, 1911)	32	204
7.	Andrew Herd (Heart of Midlothian, 1934)	32	114
8.	James Blair (Sheffield Wednesday, 1920)	31	307
9.	Archie Macauley (Brentford, 1947)	31	256
10.	Tom Tait (Sunderland, 1911)	31	174

THE LAST 10 THIRD DIVISION PLAYERS TO BE CAPPED FOR ENGLAND

1.	Steve Bull (Wolverhampton Wanderers)	1989
2.	Peter Taylor (Crystal Palace)	1976
3.	Johnny Byrne (Crystal Palace)	1961
4.	Reg Matthews (Coventry City)	1956
5.	Tommy Lawton (Notts County)	1947
6.	Joe Payne (Luton Town)	1937
7.	Albert Barrett (Fulham)	Oct 1929
8.	Len Oliver (Fulham)	May 1929
9.	Dick Hill (Millwall)	1926
10.	George Armitage (Charlton)	1925

MOST SUCCESSFUL ENGLAND MANAGERS

(to end of June 1992)

		P	W	% wins
1.	Ron Greenwood (1977-82)	55	33	60
	Alf Ramsey (1962-74)	113	68	60
3.	Walter Winterbottom (1946-62)	137	78	56
4.	Graham Taylor (1990-)	24	13	54
5.	Bobby Robson (1982-90)	95	47	49
6.	Don Revie (1974-77)	29	14	48
7.	Joe Mercer (1974)	7	3	42

This table is a bit unfair on Joe Mercer who at least tried to put a smile back on the face of the English game. That's something which a few other England managers could never have been accused of. When somebody once compiled a list of the world's shortest books, The Wit of Alf Ramsey was right near the top, while the *Guardian* described Bobby Robson as having the natural expression of a man who fears he might have left the gas on. You could say that we Scots can't talk, for was there ever a more miserable face in football than Ally MacLeod after Argentina? Poor Ally, humbled and haunted at his final press conference for that World Cup, spotted a dog sniffing around his legs. Sensing the chance for a moment of sympathy from the media, he said: 'Here I am, not a friend in the whole world except this mongrel dog.' As he bent down to pat the dog, it bit his hand!

COUNTRIES WHO HAVE REACHED MOST WORLD CUP FINAL STAGES

1.	Brazil	14
2.	Italy	12
	Germany	12
4.	Argentina	10
5.	England	9
	France	9
	Hungary	9
	Mexico	9
	Uruguay	9
10.	Belgium	8
	Czechoslovakia	8
	Spain	8
	Sweden	8
	Yugoslavia	8
15.	Scotland	7
	Soviet Union	7

Brazil, Italy and Germany have each won the trophy three times and Franz Beckenbauer has the honour of being the only man to captain and manage a World Cup winning team. He was skipper of the Germans when they beat Holland in 1974 and was manager of the victorious 1990 team. Beckenbauer was one of the all-time greats. He had such style and composure and always seemed to have so much time on the ball. Mind you, I'm not sure how good he would have looked playing for somebody like Wimbledon or Cambridge United. And he wasn't everyone's cup of tea when he had a spell in the States with New York Cosmos. One Cosmos executive was quoted as saying: 'Tell the Kraut to get his ass up front. We don't pay a million for a guy to hang around in defense.' With such tactical appreciation from the Americans, the next World Cup should be well worth looking forward to...

MOST MATCHES IN WORLD CUP FINAL STAGES

1.	Germany	68
2.	Brazil	66
3.	Italy	54
4.	Argentina	48
5.	England	41
6.	Uruguay	37
7.	France	34
8.	Yugoslavia	33
9.	Hungary	32
	Spain	32
11.	Soviet Union	31
	Sweden	31
13.	Czechoslovakia	30
14.	Mexico	29
15.	Austria	26
16.	Belgium	25
	Poland	25
18.	Chile	21
19.	Holland	20
	Scotland	20

I've mentioned the Scottish debacle in Argentina, so I think it's only fair to remind readers of one of England's greatest humiliations – that infamous 1-0 defeat by the amateurs of the United States in the 1950 World Cup. With a pre-match confidence that made Ally MacLeod look a pessimist, England were convinced that they would win comfortably, hardly surprising since their team contained names like Ramsey, Wright, Finney and Mortensen. The final score was such a shock that confused British newspaper editors thought it must have been a misprint for 1-10. And I wonder how many people know that the U.S. team which so embarrased the English included a Scotsman, McIlvenny.

COUNTRIES WHO HAVE REACHED THE WORLD CUP FINAL STAGES BUT HAVE NEVER WON A GAME

Australia
Bolivia
Bulgaria
Canada
Dutch East Indies
Egypt
El Salvador
Haiti
Honduras
Iran
Iraq
Israel
Kuwait
New Zealand
Norway
South Korea
United Arab Emirates
Zaire

Technically, the Republic of Ireland fall into this category since in Italy in 1990, they only beat Romania after penalties. The teams with the worst records are probably El Salvador, who have lost six out of six, Bulgaria, who have just six draws to show from 16 matches, and Dutch East Indies whose only game saw them lose 6-0 to Hungary in 1938. Apart from the poor old Dutch East Indies, four other teams have failed to score in the final stages – Australia, Bolivia, Canada and Zaire.

MOST GOALS IN WORLD CUP FINAL STAGES

1. Brazil — 148
2. Germany — 145
3. Italy — 89
4. Hungary — 87
5. Argentina — 82
6. France — 71
7. Uruguay — 61
8. England — 55
   Yugoslavia — 55
10. Soviet Union — 53

LEADING SCORERS IN ONE WORLD CUP TOURNAMENT

1. Just Fontaine (France, 1958) — 13
2. Sandor Kocsis (Hungary, 1954) — 11
3. Gerd Muller (West Germany, 1970) — 10
4. Eusebio (Portugal, 1966) — 9
   Ademir Marques de Menezes (Brazil, 1950) — 9
5. Leonidas da Silva (Brazil, 1938) — 8
   Guillermo Stabile (Argentina, 1930) — 8
7. Jairzinho (Brazil, 1970) — 7
   Grzegorz Lato (Poland, 1974) — 7
   Gyula Zsengeller (Hungary, 1938) — 7

The leading scorer from the home countries is Gary Lineker with six in 1986.

PLAYERS WITH MOST GOALS IN WORLD CUP FINAL STAGES (OVERALL)

1. Gerd Muller (1970, 1974)   14
2. Just Fontaine (1958)   13
3. Pele (Brazil, 1958,1962, 1966, 1970)   12
4. Sandor Kocsis (1954)   11
5. Teofilio Cubillas (Peru, 1970, 1978)   10
   Grzegorz Lato (1974, 1978, 1982)   10
   Gary Lineker (England, 1986, 1990)   10
   Helmut Rahn (West Germany, 1954, 1958)   10

PLAYERS WITH MOST APPEARANCES IN WORLD CUP FINAL STAGES

1. Uwe Seeler (West Germany, 1958, 1962, 1966, 1970) 21
   Wladislaw Zmuda (Poland, 1974, 1978, 1982, 1986)   21
3. Grzegorz Lato (Poland, 1974, 1978, 1982)   20
4. Diego Maradona (Argentina, 1982, 1986, 1990)   19
   Wolfgang Overath (West Germany, 1966, 1970, 1974) 19
   Karl-Heinz Rummenigge (West Germany) 1978,
      1982, 1986)   19
   Bertie Vogts (West Germany, 1970, 1974, 1978)   19
8. Franz Beckenbauer (West Germany, 1966, 1970,
      1974)   18
   Antonio Cabrini (Italy, 1978, 1982, 1986)   18
   Mario Kempes (Argentina, 1974, 1978, 1982)   18
   Pierre Littbarski (West Germany, 1982, 1986, 1990) 18
   Sepp Maier (West Germany, 1970, 1974, 1978)   18
   Gaetano Scirea (Italy, 1978, 1982, 1986)   18

COUNTRIES WITH MOST
REGISTERED CLUBS

1.	England	41,750
2.	Spain	30,920
3.	France	22,829
4.	West Germany	21,510
5.	Italy	20,117
6.	Japan	13,047
7.	Brazil	12,987
8.	Peru	10,000
9.	Holland	7,912
10.	Yugoslavia	7,455

The old Soviet Union had over 50,000 clubs before it was divided up into more pieces than the average wedding cake. At the other end of the scale, there are 22 clubs on the Faeroe Islands and Brunei, 17 in San Marino, 15 on Grenada, 14 on the Bahamas, eight in Qatar and seven in Liechtenstein. But if you think the leagues there might be a shade predictable, that's nothing compared to the Scilly Isles where there are just two clubs who play each other every week. I bet the Cup draw makes for compulsive viewing!

MOST SUCCESSFUL CLUBS IN EUROPE

		Trophies won
1.	Real Madrid	8
2.	Barcelona	7
3.	AC Milan	6
	Liverpool	6
5.	Ajax Amsterdam	5
6.	Bayern Munich	4
	Juventus	4
8.	Anderlecht	3
	Inter Milan	3
	Tottenham Hotspur	3
	Valencia	3

Alfredo di Stefano, the Real Madrid star of the Fifties and early Sixties, was my all time hero. And I was lucky enough to play alongside him once in a special European media team which played a South American media side at the 1978 World Cup in Argentina. As far as I was concerned, it was about the only decent thing to come out of that World Cup! We had a potentially brilliant forward line – Raymond Kopa, Just Fontaine, di Stefano, Bobby Charlton and me. We drew 5-5 but the thing that lingers longest in my memory was the sight of big Jack Charlton loping forward for free-kicks. The trouble was the brilliant Frenchman Kopa wanted to take them all himself but merely succeeded in blasting them over the bar. So Jack, who was feeling the pace a bit, had to canter back to his own half, muttering something unprintable under his breath. Three times this happened and then the fourth time, Jack yelled at me: 'Tell that … ing frog to wait until I get there.' I succeeded in restraining Kopa until Jack arrived in the box. Then Jack's brother Bobby stepped up and whacked the ball over the bar! I tell you, brotherly love was extremely strained at that point.

BRITISH CLUBS WITH MOST SEASONS IN EUROPE

(including 1992-93)

1.	Rangers	32
2.	Celtic	29
3.	Glentoran	26
4.	Linfield	23
	Liverpool	23
6.	Aberdeen	21
7.	Dundee United	19
8.	Hibernian	16
	Manchester United	16
	Shamrock Rovers	16

COUNTRIES WITH MOST EUROPEAN TROPHIES

(European Cup, Cup Winners' Cup, Fairs/UEFA Cup)

1.	England	23
2.	Spain	20
3.	Italy	17
4.	West Germany	12
5.	Holland	9
6.	Belgium	4
	Portugal	4
8.	Scotland	3
	Soviet Union	3
10.	Sweden	2
	Yugoslavia	2

THE 10 MOST SUCCESSFUL NORTHERN IRELAND CLUBS

(League, Ulster Cup, Gold Cup, Irish Cup)

		Trophies won
1.	Linfield	86
2.	Glentoran	48
3.	Belfast Celtic	17
4.	Coleraine	14
5.	Glenavon	11
6.	Distillery	8
7.	Ards	7
	Ballymena	7
	Crusaders	7
	Portadown	7

THE 10 MOST SUCCESSFUL REPUBLIC OF IRELAND CLUBS

(League and Cup)

		Trophies won
1.	Shamrock Rovers	37
2.	Dundalk	16
3.	Bohemians	12
4.	Shelbourne	11
5.	Drumcondra	10
6.	Waterford	8
7.	Cork United	7
8.	St Patrick's Athletic	6
9.	Cork Athletic	4
	Limerick	4
	St James's Gate	4

Derry City, who switched from the Irish League to the League of Ireland, have won seven trophies in all (five in the north and two in the south).

THE 10 MOST SUCCESSFUL WEST GERMAN CLUBS

(League and Cup)

		Trophies won
1.	Bayern Munich	20
2.	IFC Nuremberg	12
3.	Schalke 04	9
	SV Hamburg	9
5.	Borussia Moenchengladbach	7
	IFC Cologne	7
7.	VfB Stuttgart	6
8.	Borussia Dortmund	5
	Eintracht Frankfurt	5
10.	Dresden SC	4
	IFC Kaiserslauten	4
	VfB Leipzig	4
	Werder Bremen	4

THE 10 MOST SUCCESSFUL ITALIAN CLUBS

(League and Cup)

		Trophies won
1.	Juventus	30
2.	AC Milan	16
	Inter-Milan	16
4.	Torino	12
5.	Genoa	10
6.	Bologna	9
	AS Roma	9
8.	Pro Vercelli	7
9.	Fiorentina	6
10.	Napoli	5

THE 10 MOST SUCCESSFUL FRENCH CLUBS

(League and Cup)

		Trophies won
1.	Olympique Marseille	18
2.	Saint Etienne	16
3.	AS Monaco	10
4.	Lille OSC	8
	Stade de Reims	8
6.	Girondins Bordeaux	7
7	Nantes	7
8.	OGC Nice	6
	Racing Club Paris	6
10.	Red Star	5

When Marseille won the 1992 French League title, it meant that Trevor Steven had won championship medals in three different countries – with Everton, Rangers and Marseille. Now he's back in Scotland. At this rate, he'll soon have been to more countries than Alan Whicker.

THE 10 MOST SUCCESSFUL DUTCH CLUBS

(League and Cup)

		Trophies won
1.	Ajax Amsterdam	34
2.	Feyenoord	21
3.	PSV Eindhoven	20
4.	HVV The Hague	9
	Sparta Rotterdam	9
6.	HBS The Hague	5
	Quick The Hague	5
	Willem II Tilburg	5
9.	AZ 67 Alkmaar	4
	Go Ahead Deventer	4
	RCH Haarlem	4

THE 10 MOST SUCCESSFUL SPANISH CLUBS

(League and Cup)

		Trophies won
1.	Real Madrid	41
2.	Barcelona	34
3.	Athletic Bilbao	31
4.	Atletico Madrid	16
5.	Valencia	9
6.	Seville	4
7.	Real Sociedad	3
	Real Union de Irun	3
	Real Zaragoza	3
10.	Espanol	2
	Real Betis	2

CHAPTER NINE

ODDBALLS

THE TOP 10 SOCCER SONGS

	Highest UK chart placing	
1. Back Home (England World Cup Squad)	1	1970
World in Motion (England New Order)	1	1990
3. This Time (England World Cup Squad)	2	1982
4. Anfield Rap (Liverpool FC)	3	1988
5. Ole Ola (Rod Stewart and Scotland World Cup Squad)	4	1978
6. Blue is the Colour (Chelsea FC)	5	1972
Ossie's Dream (Spurs Cup Final Squad)	5	1981
We Have a Dream (Scotland World Cup Squad)	5	1982
9. Leeds United (Leeds United FC)	10	1972
We All Follow Man Utd (Manchester Utd FC)	10	1985

Oh dear. There are some real horrors here, some that wouldn't even be considered good enough to make the Norwegian entry for the Eurovision Song Contest. But I do detect a glimmer of hope on the horizon for it seems that the days of the dreaded singalong are on the wane. Time was when the first thing a club did on reaching Wembley was to book a recording studio but in the last few years the number of these dire ditties has decreased considerably. And that's got to be good news for everyone who isn't hard of hearing.

10 PLAYERS' FIRST JOBS

Chris Waddle – sausage seasoning maker
Ian Wright – plasterer
Steve Bull – warehouse worker
Bruce Grobbelaar – jungle fighter
Vinny Jones – hod-carrier
Kerry Dixon – tool-maker
Kevin Keegan – storeroom clerk
Peter Beardsley – labourer in a ship valve factory
Iain Dowie – design engineer with British Aerospace
Stanley Matthews – office boy at Stoke City

Chris Waddle was 16 when he landed a £20-a-week job with Cheviot Seasoning Ltd of Sunderland, making seasoning to flavour sausages and pies. He stayed there for two and a half years and the high spot was being allowed to drive the fork lift. But the majority of his time was spent standing at the foot of the blender, judging when sufficient seasoning mixture had flowed down to fill a 56 lb. box, or sweeping up or glueing boxes together. The worst thing was that the smell of the dust began to get down Chris's throat. He used to go home and spit red phlegm. 'Eventually they gave me a mask,' he says, 'but it made me look like Miss Piggy.' It's a wonder Chris got the job at all because he went for the interview on the back of his brother's motor bike but couldn't get his crash helmet off. So he sat through the entire interview wearing a crash helmet!

THE FIRST 5 GAMES ON MATCH OF THE DAY

1. Liverpool 3, Arsenal 2   (22 August, 1964)
2. Chelsea 3, Sunderland 1   (29 August, 1964)
3. Fulham 2, Manchester United 1   (5 September, 1964)
4. West Ham United 3,
         Tottenham Hotspur 2   (12 September, 1964)
5. Chelsea 2, Leeds United 0   (19 September, 1964)

Match of the Day began on BBC2 which was initially confined to the London area. This meant that for the first match, there were more spectators at Anfield than there were viewers of the programme. That debut fixture launched a star too when a cat ran on to the pitch in the middle of play. Arsenal had also featured in the very first match ever to be televised, when they beat Everton 3-2 back in 1936. Although part of the 1937 FA Cup final between Sunderland and Preston was screened, the first final to be televised in its entirety was Preston versus Huddersfield in 1938. Every subsequent final has been shown live except for the 1952 Arsenal-Newcastle game for which the Football Association refused to give permission for television coverage. Incidentally, the first FA Cup tie, other than the final, to be televised was the 1947 fifth round tie between Charlton Athletic and Blackburn Rovers. Charlton marked the occasion by winning 1-0, en route to lifting the trophy itself. The results services on both channels are extremely efficient these days but when Grandstand started in 1958, they had a few teething troubles. They once baffled pools hopefuls by inadvertantly giving out the half-times as final scores and on the very first edition, they couldn't stay for some of the results since the Lone Ranger was waiting...

THE 10 COMMONEST PLAYING INJURIES

1.	Twists and sprains	52%
2.	Bruises	17%
3.	Fractures	8%
	Tears	8%
5.	Inflammations	6%
6.	Cuts and lacerations	4%
7.	Concussions	2%
	Dislocations	2%
	Other injuries	2%
10.	Abrasions	under 1%

I think the tears that the doctors who carried out this extensive research had in mind were things like torn ligaments rather than the kind shed by Paul Gascoigne. When everybody started talking about Gazza tears at the last World Cup, Greavsie thought they were on about road atlases!

10 CLUBS WHO HAVE BEEN SPONSORED BY ALCOHOL

Blackburn Rovers (McEwans Lager)
Cork City (Guinness)
Nottingham Forest (Shipstones)
Notts County (Home Ales)
St Johnstone (The Famous Grouse)
Stockport County (Cobra Lager)
Stoke City (Ansells)
Sunderland (Vaux)
Tottenham Hotspur (Holsten)
Wrexham (Marstons)

The BBC had difficulty in coming to terms with shirt sponsorship. For any game featured on Match of the Day, teams had to wear plain shirts without their sponsors' names. In 1981, Everton goalkeeper Jim McDonagh mistakenly wore his jersey with the name of the club's sponsors, Hafnia, emblazoned across it for the second half of the televised game with Crystal Palace. So when it was shown on Match of the Day that night, viewers saw McDonagh from a side-angle only in the second half.

25 FAMOUS FANS

Jeffrey Archer (Bristol Rovers)
Danny Baker (Millwall)
Melvyn Bragg (Arsenal)
Tommy Cannon (Rochdale)
Jasper Carrott (Birmingham City)
Sebastian Coe (Chelsea)
Tom Courtenay (Hull City)
Steve Cram (Sunderland)
Paul Daniels (Doncaster Rovers)

David Frost (Norwich City)
David Hamilton (Fulham)
Rt Hon. Roy Hattersley, MP (Sheffield Wednesday)
James Herriott (Sunderland)
Cardinal Basil Hume (Newcastle United)
David Jensen (Crystal Palace)
Nigel Kennedy (Aston Villa)
Robert Kilroy-Silk (Liverpool)
John Leslie (Hibernian)
Rt Hon. John Major, MP (Chelsea)
Ian McShane (Manchester United)
Robert Plant (Wolverhampton Wanderers)
Su Pollard (Nottingham Forest)
Delia Smith (Norwich City)
June Whitfield (Wimbledon)
Mike Yarwood (Stockport County)

Ian McShane's dad Harry once played for Manchester United while Steve Cram also used parental influence to further his support for Sunderland. When the Roker men won the FA Cup in 1973, they took it on a tour of the area but a few of them got slightly the worse for wear. So for safe keeping, the Cup was taken into police custody. Steve's dad was a policeman and when the trophy landed at his station, he got straight on to the phone to his son and said: 'We've got the FA Cup here, quick get down and have your photo taken with it.' And that's how a 12-year-old Steve Cram came to get his photo taken with the FA Cup. Actor Tom Courtenay named his dog Wagstaff after Hull City's prolific striker of the Sixties, Ken Wagstaff. What a great name for a dog. Meanwhile Jasper Carrott has never made any secret of the suffering associated with supporting Birmingham City. During a particularly bad run, he shrugged it off with: 'Some you lose, some you draw.'

LEADING WOMEN'S TEAMS IN ENGLAND

(Based on final National League placings 1991-92)

1. Doncaster Belles
2. Knowsley United
3. Notts Rangers
4. Ipswich Town
5. Millwall Lionesses
6. Wimbledon
7. Red Star Southampton
8. Maidstone Tigresses

Doncaster Belles are certainly the most successful women's team in the country over recent years. Since 1983, they have won the Women's FA Cup on four occasions and been runners-up on another four. Their total number of victories in that competition is only bettered by Southampton who won the trophy eight times in its first 11 years, between 1971 and 1981. All things considered, I would have thought there was a pretty good case for them to swap places with Doncaster Rovers. I can just hear Third Division managers moaning about The Belles! The Belles!

BEST SELLING SUBBUTEO TEAMS

(Based on 1991 figures)

1. England
2. Liverpool
3. Manchester United
4. Tottenham Hotspur
5. Arsenal
6. Germany

7. Brazil
8. Leeds United
9. Liverpool second strip
10. Aston Villa
11. Scotland
12. Manchester United second strip
13. Everton
14. Norwich City
15. Celtic

C an any feeling in football compare to the despair when John Barnes goes up the vacuum cleaner or the dog chews Ian Rush's head? Mind, it never goes anywhere near the Tommy Smith figure... Smithy was a determined character on the park. If there was a danger man on the other side, Shanks would tell Smithy before the game: 'Go in and shake his bones.' And he did.

BEST SELLING SUBBUTEO
ACCESSORIES

1. Referee and linesmen
2. Mitre footballs
3. Scoreboard
4. Trainers bench
5. Throw-in figures
6. Corner kick figures
7. FA Cup
8. Adidas footballs
9. Italia footballs
10. Italia goals

15 SOCCER INNOVATIONS

1866   Duration of game fixed at 90 minutes
1872   Introduction of corner kick
1872   Size of ball fixed
1874   Shinguards introduced
1875   Crossbar replaces length of tape
1875   Teams change ends only at half-time, not after every
       goal
1878   Referee's whistle introduced
1882   Two-handed throw-in introduced
1891   The penalty kick arrives
1891   The first goal nets
1939   Numbering becomes compulsory in the Football
       League
1951   The white ball comes into official use
1965   One substitute allowed for an injured player – and for
       any reason a year later. Two substitutes permitted
       from 1986
1981   Football League brings in three points for a win
1987   Play-offs re-introduced in the Football League

Love them or hate them, penalty shoot-outs have become part and parcel of the modern game. The first time a shoot-out was used between two senior British clubs was in the 1970 Watney Cup when Manchester United defeated Hull City 4-3 on penalties after drawing 1-1. The longest shoot-out was for an Argentina League game in 1988 between Argentinos Juniors and Racing Club. No fewer than 44 spot-kicks had to be taken before a winner emerged, Argentinos finally winning 20-19.

TOP 20 MATCH-DAY PROGRAMMES IN THE FOOTBALL LEAGUE

(Based on 1991-92 awards run by *Match* magazine and the Commercial Managers Association)

1. Aston Villa
2. Everton
3. Tottenham Hotspur
   Derby County
5. West Ham United
6. Leeds United
7. Manchester City
8. Norwich City
9. Chelsea
10. Ipswich Town
11. Queen's Park Rangers
12. Sheffield Wednesday
13. West Bromwich Albion
14. Leicester City
15. Tranmere Rovers
16. Coventry City
17. Wrexham
18. Liverpool
    Middlesbrough
20. Watford

Other club programmes which received special mentions were Brighton & Hove Albion (Most Improved Programme in Division Two), Birmingham City and Fulham (joint runners-up in Division Three), Hartlepool (Most Improved Programme in Division Three), Lincoln City (runners-up in Division Four), York City (third in Division Four) and Cardiff City (Most Improved Programme in Division Four).

20 SOCCER FILMS

The Winning Goal (GB, 1920)
Up for the Cup (GB, 1931)
The Arsenal Stadium Mystery (GB, 1939)
Women Who Have Run Off-Side (Czechoslovakia, 1951)
The Football Parson (Denmark, 1951)
The Great Game (GB, 1953)
The Goalkeeper Lives in our Street (Czechoslovakia, 1957)
Comrade President the Centre-Forward (Yugoslavia, 1962)
Ivana in the Forward Line (Czechoslovakia, 1963)
Let's Go Wakadaisho (Japan, 1967)
Fish, Football and Girls (Israel, 1968)
The Goalkeeper's Fear of the Penalty (FRG/Austria, 1971)
Football of the Good Old Days (Hungary, 1973)
Striker (India, 1978)
Yesterday's Hero (GB, 1979)
Gregory's Girl (GB, 1981)
Escape to Victory (US, 1981)
Those Glory, Glory Days (GB, 1983)
Excuse Me – Are You Watching Football? (GDR, 1983)
A Mort L'Arbitre (France, 1984)

Some corkers here, including Manchester United freak Ian McShane as a brilliant footballer gone to ruin (wonder who could have inspired that?) in *Yesterday's Hero*; Diana Dors and Thora Hird (an unlikely combination if ever there was one) in *The Great Game*; Danny Blanchflower making a guest appearance in *Those Glory, Glory Days*; and Pelé doing the same in a 1983 American movie, *Young Giants*. *Up for the Cup* was one of the earliest British soccer films, a jolly farce about a Yorkshireman who landed in hot water when he came to London for the Cup final. But for sheer drama, what could compare with *The Arsenal Stadium Mystery*, the torrid tale of a footballer poisoned during a match? I reckon the agent did it.

FANZINE TITLES

Never Loved Ellis (Aston Villa)
The Ugly Duckling (Aylesbury United)
Revenge of the Killer Penguin (Bath City)
Bee-Sotted (Brentford)
Where Were You At The Shay? (Bury)
The Abbey Rabbit (Cambridge United)
The Cumberland Sausage (Carlisle United)
The Onion Bag (Chester City)
Clyde-O-Scope (Clyde)
Champion Hill Street Blues (Dulwich Hamlet)
Talk Of The Town End (Enfield)
The Loonatic (Forfar Athletic)
There's Only One F In Fulham (Fulham)
Sing When We're Fishing (Grimsby Town)
Always the Bridesmaid (Heart of Midlothian)
A Load Of Cobbolds (Ipswich Town)
The Hanging Sheep (Leeds United)
D Pleated (Luton Town)
Show Me The Way To Go Home (Maidstone United)
Mr. Bismarck's Electric Pickelhaube (Meadowbank Thistle)
Dial M For Merthyr (Merthyr Tydfil)
The Almighty Brian (Nottingham Forest)
Worse Than East Fife (Partick Thistle)
Frattonise (Portsmouth)
The Memoirs of Seth Bottomley (Port Vale)
A Nightmare On Terregles Street (Queen Of The South)
A Kick Up The Rs (Queen's Park Rangers)
Taking the Biscuit (Reading)
Mi Whippet's Dead (Rotherham United)
Old McDiarmid Had A Farm (St Johnstone)
Rebels Without a Clue (Slough Town)
The Pies Were Cold (Telford United)
Bamber's Right Foot (Torquay United)
A Load of Bull (Wolverhampton Wanderers)
Reliant Robin (Wrexham)

CLUBS WITH MOST APPEARANCES ON THE MATCH

(to end of 1991-92)

1.	Liverpool	26
2.	Manchester United	23
3.	Arsenal	19
4.	Nottingham Forest	16
	Tottenham Hotspur	16
6.	Everton	12
7.	Leeds United	11
8.	Aston Villa	8
9.	Manchester City	5
	Norwich City	5
11.	Coventry City	4
	Sheffield Wednesday	4
13.	Chelsea	3
	West Ham United	3
14.	Millwall	2
	Southampton	2

The first Football League game to be televised live was Blackpool v Bolton Wanderers in 1960. It was intended to be the forerunner of a regular Friday night soccer programme on TV but unfortunately the 1-0 win to Bolton was so dull that plans for covering further games were swiftly dropped.

8 FORMER FOOTBALLERS

Stan Boardman
Julio Iglesias
Eddie Large
Glen Murphy
Des O'Connor
Brian Regan
Rod Stewart
Charlie Williams

Comedian Stan Boardman and Brookside star Brian Regan could both have ended up playing for Liverpool. Stan was a centre-half with the 'A' team and Brian was a promising young goalkeeper. Glen Murphy from London's Burning was a forward on Charlton's books while both Julio Iglesias and Eddie Large saw their careers wrecked by injury. Julio was goalkeeper with Real Madrid's reserve team but a car crash ended his playing days, and Eddie was, in slimmer times, a midfield dynamo with his beloved Manchester City. But when he was 15, he fell off his bike and a bus ran over his ankles. Comedian Charlie Williams had a reputation as a bit of a hard man with Doncaster Rovers in the Fifties and 16-year-old Rod Stewart was an apprentice with Brentford. He was paid £8 a week but, fed up with cleaning the first teamers' boots, packed it in after three weeks, never having kicked a ball. Rod then moved on to a job which he thought was a lot livelier than playing for Brentford – he became a gravedigger. And how many people know that young Des O'Connor was once a winger with Northampton Town? I bet they were glad they never got to Wembley and had to release a Cup final song...

189

COMMENTATORS' CHOICE

Dickie Davies (Southampton)
Desmond Lynam (Brighton & Hove Albion)
Brian Moore (Gillingham)
John Motson (Spurs and Boston United)
Nick Owen (Luton Town)
Alan Parry (Liverpool and Wycombe Wanderers)
Jonathan Powell (Swindon Town)
Steve Rider (Charlton Athletic)
Jim Rosenthal (Oxford United)
Alan Weeks (Brighton & Hove Albion)
Bob Wilson (Arsenal)
Julian Wilson (Swindon Town)

We all try to be impartial but the above are not afraid to wear their hearts on their sleeves. Alan Parry is even a director at Wycombe. But for first-hand experience, how many can compare with David Coleman who, in his days as a young journalist in Cheshire, went along to cover Stockport County Reserves? When he arrived at Edgeley Park, Coleman, a champion miler, found that County were a man short. And they asked him to make up the numbers. I wonder what sort of write-up he gave himself.

10 THINGS COMMENTATORS AND PUNDITS WISH THEY HAD NEVER SAID

'Gary Lineker has now scored 37 goals. That is precisely twice as many as last year.' – John Motson

'I'd like to have seen Tony Morley left on as a down and out winger.' – Jimmy Armfield

'Real possession football this...and Zico's lost it.' – John Helm

'And for those of you watching who haven't got television sets, live commentary is on Radio 2.' – David Coleman

'The last player to score a hat-trick in a Cup final was Stan Mortensen. He even had a final named after him – the

Matthews final.' – Lawrie McMenemy

'More football in a moment – but first highlights of the Scottish League Cup Final.' – Gary Newbon

'I have other irons in the fire, but I'm keeping them close to my chest.' – John Bond

'Maradona gets tremendous elevation with his balls no matter what position he's in.' – David Pleat

'Don't tell those coming in now the result of that fantastic match. Now let's have another look at Italy's winning goal.' – David Coleman

'For the benefit of those watching in black and white, Spurs are the ones in the yellow shirts.' – John Motson

Live television can be a harrowing ordeal, particularly when you're starting out. It was nerve-wracking enough for me, I can tell you, and for Bob Wilson. I don't think Bob will ever forget his first match report at the end of an edition of Grandstand. He went to cover Arsenal v Manchester United and was terrified about rushing back to the studio to give his story. He had been told to drum the first line into his head and repeat it over and over again, then the rest would flow. So on his way back to the studio, he rehearsed: 'I've just got back from Highbury where Arsenal beat Manchester United by two goals to nil and Alan Ball was the star of the match.' He reached the studio, sat down in his seat, barely had time to draw breath and then listened aghast as Frank Bough introduced him: 'Here's Bob Wilson who's just come back from Highbury where Arsenal beat Manchester United by two goals to nil and it seems Alan Ball was the star of the match. That right, Bob…?'